SOUL
ANCHORS

SOUL
ANCHORS
CHRISSIE TOMLINSON

TATE PUBLISHING
AND ENTERPRISES, LLC

Published by Tate Publishing & Enterprises, LLC
127 E. Trade Center Terrace | Mustang, Oklahoma 73064 USA
1.888.361.9473 | www.tatepublishing.com

Tate Publishing is committed to excellence in the publishing industry. The company reflects the philosophy established by the founders, based on Psalm 68:11,

"The Lord gave the word and great was the company of those who published it."

Book design copyright © 2016 by Tate Publishing, LLC. All rights reserved.
Cover design by Albert Ceasar Compay
Interior design by Manolito Bastasa

Published in the United States of America

ISBN: 978-1-68319-314-2
Religion / Devotional
16.03.02

We Have an Anchor

Will your anchor hold in the storms of life,
When the clouds unfold their wings of strife?
When the strong tides lift and the cables strain,
Will your anchor drift, or firm remain?

It is safely moored, 'twill the storm withstand,
For 'tis well secured by the Savior's hand;
And the cables, passed from His heart to mine,
Can defy that blast, thro' strength divine.

It will surely hold in the Straits of Fear—
When the breakers have told that the reef is near;
Though the tempest rave and the wild winds blow,
Not an angry wave shall our bark o'erflow.

It will firmly hold in the Floods of Death—
When the waters cold chill our latest breath,
On the rising tide it can never fail,
While our hopes abide within the Veil.

When our eyes behold through the gath'ring night
The city of gold, our harbor bright,
We shall anchor fast by the heav'nly shore,
With the storms all past forevermore.

We have an anchor that keeps the soul
Steadfast and sure while the billows roll,
Fastened to the Rock which cannot move,
Grounded firm and deep in the Savior's love.

—William J. Kirkpatrick

Acknowledgments

I WOULD LIKE to express my deepest gratitude to my dear friends and sisters in Christ who have been so transparent in sharing their testimonies—Windie, Sonya, Elizabeth, Robyn, Jaime, Jackie, and Kim. These ladies shared their stories from the depths of their hearts with the hope that their journeys will encourage others. I'm grateful for their willingness to minister in this way.

I also am so grateful for my sweet friend and co-laborer in words, Debi Hutchens (*A Bypass in the Road: Journey of the Heart; Got a Hole in the Bottom of My Shoe, But It Is Well with My "Sole")* for her encouragement and for praying me through this effort.

I'm also very appreciative of Terri DeFoor and Dr. Allen Hughes for lending their editing talents to this project—what a difference their input has made in the final product.

Finally, my gratitude goes to a dear friend, Lisa Mills (lisaoutloud.net), who took time during a very busy season of ministry to contribute to this project. Lisa is an inspiration, and I'm forever thankful for her friendship and encouragement.

Contents

Foreword

I THINK MOST people would agree that in today's world of busyness and impatience, our time spent in God's Word is somewhat lacking. For the average person, having more resources and better technology at our fingertips somehow does not give us more access to dig deeper into the Scriptures that hold the very heart of God. Why is that? I believe many people assume that the Bible is irrelevant to our modern lives or that it is too difficult to interpret and understand. We reserve the joy of discovering the beautiful truths and hidden treasures of God's Word for those who are educated, ordained, or do I dare say, "more spiritual" than the rest of us. This could not be more of a disservice to our lives, families, and souls.

For those who know this all too well, there is a deep desire to not only know the Scriptures for themselves, but for others to read God's word with understanding and live out its life-changing truths. I first realized that Chrissie Tomlinson was one of these people when I had the privilege of meeting her at a conference where I was speaking.

It's hard to pinpoint exactly what it is that's instantly warm and familiar about Chrissie. Do you know that feeling you have when you are curled up in your favorite pajamas, warm coffee in hand, and your favorite candle burning tableside? Well, being with Chrissie is a lot like having that feeling. She exudes a love that is safe, honest, and real. As I've gotten to know her even more, I was in no way shocked when she revealed her desire to write this book. My only thought was, *When will it be finished, and how soon can I get it?*

These pages are such a breath of fresh air—although breath of salt air may be more accurate. Each paragraph encourages you to dive deeper, and each chapter leaves a craving for the next. *Soul Anchors* is such a practical answer to the tough questions of growing in our faith as we move through the ups and downs of a real relationship with Christ. Through this Bible study, Chrissie shares her personal experiences of knowing and trusting the Anchor of her soul more each day. I believe, because of this intertwined strength and loveliness that we come to know as Chrissie's determination and testimony, you will be even more resolved to know Christ as the Anchor for your own life.

If you've ever longed to know the Creator of the universe in a more personal way, then I pray that journeying through this Bible study will inspire you to launch out into the deep of His Word where He reveals Himself best. Go ahead, dive into His promises, jump headfirst into His grace, and rest in knowing that to swim in the deep of His love is to also be anchored at the soul.

—Lisa Mills
Author of *Lord, Did I Really Shave My Legs for This?*

Soul Anchors

It's a crazy, unpredictable life in a crazy, unpredictable world. Most days, we feel as if we are spinning around in a whirlwind that takes our breath and refuses to give it back. Then God provides sweet moments of grace for us to finally experience the calmness of those promised still waters we long for, but it seems it is just for a moment. Soon the craziness starts up again.

For me, the craziness usually starts with something mundane like the "maintenance required" light coming on in my car. From the moment that light comes on, I'm reminded of how hard it is to find time in my schedule to take my car in for servicing. I know that not servicing my car regularly can lead to more inconvenient experiences; breakdowns never happen at a good time! But this maintenance light just seems to be one of those things that the more it blinks at me, the more other tasks come up that I have to deal with, and deal with now! How can something so simple make me feel so unsettled?

Other times, it isn't the normal craziness of life but the devastation of loss. Sometimes, it's the fear that living in this uncertain world carries with it—the fear of not meeting bills, of losing a job, of worrying that a spouse is drawing away; the fear of illness when something doesn't look quite right to the doctor. For some, it is the fear of growing old or perhaps of being alone. Just waking up in the morning can sometimes throw us into a world where it seems that there is nothing firm to hold on to.

This world holds no sense of true security for us, and sometimes it is easier to succumb to feelings of insecurity than to try to summon the strength to be women of courage in the face of the struggles that we face. Thankfully, though, God's Word tells us that even though this world is definitely a place of trouble, Christ has overcome it; and because He has, we have something to hold onto. And even in those times when we can't hold on any longer, He—our Anchor—is holding on to us with His ever-present Spirit and with the soul anchors He provides to His children.

Isaiah 43 is a great passage of assurance for God's people. He tells us, "Fear not, for I have redeemed you; I have called you by name, you are mine. When you pass through the waters, I will be with you; and through the rivers, they shall not overwhelm you....because you are precious in my eyes, and honored, and I love you." In this passage, we are assured of His love for us. We are reminded of the freedom that we have through His redemption and of the peace that we have as He abolishes all our fears—all wrapped up in the truth of the Word He has so graciously and mercifully given to us.

These soul anchors—love, truth, peace, freedom—are anchors that are unchangeable despite the circumstances, despite our feelings, and despite all the obstacles that are thrown into our paths. These anchors hold us in place and hold us together.

This book was born from a series of Bible studies written for a ladies' retreat. The retreat came at a season in the life of the hosting church where it seemed, from the outside, that there wasn't a strong sense of hope and security. But when the hurts and frustrations were peeled back, there was the very hand of God holding all things together. As you read some of their stories, you will see pure evidence that Christ Himself is serving as the anchor for the soul of this church and for the sweet people struggling to hold on, to love and serve one another, to seek reconciliation and right wrongs despite the stormy winds blowing against it, seeking to rest in the very truth of God's Word and experience fully the freedom that is found in the gracious and lavish gift of salvation. I am convinced that what these women have experienced and are experiencing is quite common in our culture today, and that the message of their struggles and successes will resonate with each one of us in a way that will bring strength, encouragement, and a deep sense of fellowship.

It's a crazy, crazy life in a crazy, crazy world. And on those days that make you feel more insecure than others, what is it that gives you that sense of security that you are being held? What grounds you and gives you the hope and confidence to keep moving forward, to pick yourself up when you've fallen down? The definition of the term "anchor" carries with it several connotations that make it a perfect symbol for the things that we hold on to in this life.

An anchor is something that restricts the movement of a floating vessel, and it does this by holding firmly to an unmoving object, like the bottom of the sea. Second, an anchor provides security by pulling one structure, with the perfect amount of tension, into another structure, as seen in suspension bridges. An anchor is also defined as something that binds one part of a structure to another part. And last, an anchor is generally defined as a person or thing that can be counted on for security or stability or support. For me, an anchor is something that is stronger than myself that I can lean into when life's winds are blowing so hard I don't think I can stand on my own. Do any of those definitions sound familiar to you? Do they sound like something you may be looking for?

Each chapter of this book is composed of two parts. The first is the text of the book and includes a look at Scriptures related to each of the anchors we are examining as well as the personal testimonies from ladies who have experienced the security found in trusting our Anchor, Jesus Christ. Following this section in each chapter is a second section called "Learn It and Live It." This section gives you the opportunity to dig a little deeper into the Bible content and helps you to find a more personal connection and application with the topic. I encourage you to really take your time with this part. It's not a race! Even if you take a day or two and only cover a couple of questions, that's okay. The point is for you to understand how to take God's Word and really put it into action in your life. A good idea is to find a friend or two who will be your accountability partners and who will go through the study with you. Find a time each week or maybe every two weeks and discuss your responses to the "Learn It and Live It" section. If you are leading a study group, leaders' guides are available for free download at ChrissieTomlinson7.wordpress.com.

As we examine the anchors we have through Christ, my hope and my prayer is that we will gain the strength and the confidence we need to continue on our journey with grace, always upholding one another and holding increasingly tighter to the hand of our Savior.

Learn It and Live It: Introduction

What do you hope to learn or to gain by completing this study?

_____

_____

_____

_____

_____

Are there areas of your life where you feel insecure? What are they? What causes you to feel this insecurity?

_____

_____

_____

_____

_____

What is your definition of the term "anchor?"

_____

_____

_____

_____

_____

Describe a season in your life when it was very clear to you that Christ was your anchor?

_____

_____

_____

_____

_____

Anchored by Love

DO YOU EVER have those days when you feel you accidentally put on your invisibility cloak when you got up that morning? Days when you feel completely ignored or overlooked?

Recently, I was having dinner at a restaurant with a friend of mine when a gentleman came in with his family. My friend and the gentleman were coworkers, so he approached the table and they greeted one another and then proceeded to carry on a conversation with each other. The gentleman never acknowledged that I was sitting there, and when I made an effort to introduce myself, he ignored me, turning so that he was completely facing away from me. That, it seems, was one of those times when my invisibility cloak was successfully activated!

Now, granted, this gentleman likely did not intend to make me feel demeaned; and likely, he didn't even realize that he was ignoring me. Most likely, it was just my allowing a situation to cause me to question my worth. But when so many of us already question ourselves, our worth, and our value, situations like these can really break us down and solidify those self-doubts that are so difficult to tamp down.

We all need to feel loved and accepted. Sadly, though, a lot of people are lonely these days, and a lot of people feel unloved and unvalued. It is easy to feel as if we are just drifting through life, merely existing from day to day without purpose. Love is such an important anchor in our lives, connecting us to God and to others; yet it is one that so many people feel is out of their reach, mainly because so many of us lack a good understanding of what love really is.

If someone were to ask you what it means to experience true love, what would you say? How would you describe what true love looks like? Would you share an example from your own life? Would you talk about how you would really like to be truly loved but have never really experienced it? How do we know what true love looks like when it seems that we so seldom see it in this world? And how do we find it in ourselves to love others when we don't feel loved ourselves?

Jesus gave many examples of what love looks like. In John 13:3–5, we read, "Jesus, knowing that the Father had given all things into His hands, and that He had come from God and was going back to God, rose from supper. He laid aside His outer garments, and taking a towel, tied it around His waist. Then He poured water into a basin and began to wash the disciples' feet and to wipe them with the towel that was wrapped around Him."

So many thoughts come to mind when I read these verses. That Christ would choose to express His love to His disciples through the washing of their feet is today, as it was at that time, a revolutionary concept. In this act, He shows the centrality of humility, grace, and kindness in the way that we love others. He shows that no task is too menial, that no person is too great, and that no person is insignificant. He shows that a true expression of our love for others involves putting aside everything we believe to be true about ourselves, other than the fact that we are His, and that our love for Him should overflow into our willingness to lower ourselves to serve others.

There was no guilt trip here. Jesus didn't say, "Well, since none of you are going to do this, I suppose I will have to. Of course I should have known. I have to do all the dirty work around here." I'm sure He didn't even think this to Himself, even though He had every right to! There was no false humility here, no hidden agenda. He acted out of the purest of loves, with the purest of motives.

According to verse 3, Jesus knew that God had given all things into His hands. He was fully aware of His sovereignty, of His deity. Yet rather than blind the disciples with His infinite and radiant glory, He humbled Himself. He made Himself nothing and took on the form of a servant (Phil. 2:6–8) so that He could instruct His disciples in the kind of love He expected them to show to one another. In verses 13–15, He tells them, "You call me Teacher and Lord, and you are right…If I then have washed your feet, you also ought to wash one another's feet. For I have given you an example that you also should do just as I have done to you."

Interestingly enough, Jesus knew the ultimate expression of His love was not in washing the disciples' feet. He knew ultimately He would go to the cross and then to the grave, completely and willingly emptying Himself of His glory. He later said that there is no greater love than for a man to lay down his life for his friends (John 15). However, at this point, all Jesus was asking of His disciples was their willingness to put aside their natural tendency to one-up each other and their sense of selfish ambitions and be willing to serve each other no matter what the need. In 1 John 3:16–17, we read, "By this we know love, that He laid down His life for us, and we ought to lay down our lives for the brethren. But whoever has the world's goods and sees his brother in need, and closes his heart against him, how does the love of God abide in him? Little children, let us not love with word or with tongue but in deed and truth."

The fact that we live in a world where this kind of love is a rarity is blatantly evident all around us. You only have to take a short ride from where most of us live to see the plight of people who are in need, who are lonely, who are hurting, people who need to be shown love and kindness in the form of a helping hand. But those are not the only evidences of a culture whose mind-set is clearly "me-focused." How often do we encounter impatient people at stores, restaurants, and other businesses? How many car accidents are attributed to drivers who are too impatient to slow down?

The truth of the matter is that so many women don't really have a problem with sincerely acting with this servant heart toward others. Most of us have an uncanny ability to sense the needs of others and find ways to meet those needs. And moreover, we are not only willing but also seem to be naturally able to overlook our own needs and personal comfort to serve others. This can get us into trouble if we are not careful to keep our motives pure; just because we are willing to serve does not mean that we are willing to love. Serving requires us to give our time, our energy, and our skill. But loving requires us to give ourselves—a very risky prospect, but one which is at the heart of what Jesus is calling us to do.

Another example of what love looks like is the familiar story of Jesus's visit with Mary and Martha, recorded in Luke 10:38–42. Scriptures tell us that these two sisters had two different approaches to welcoming the Savior into their home. Mary sat at His feet, listening to Him. Martha was distracted with preparing a meal for Jesus. The way the word picture plays out is that Martha was banging around the kitchen, more than a little put out that she was having to do all the work alone while her sister sat uselessly around, certainly not an accepted behavior for a woman in the home in those days. Finally, Martha got tired of being the "good" sister (good being defined as "busy") and petulantly sought support from Jesus.

Jesus's gentle correction pointed out a really powerful lesson on what love is to look like. He said, "Martha, Martha, you are worried and bothered about so many things; but only one thing is necessary. For Mary has chosen the good part, which shall not be taken away from her" (v. 41–42).

Wait, didn't we just read that Jesus's example was to love by serving? Isn't this what Martha was doing? There are a couple of things to see here. First, I think it has kind of been programmed into us that working in the kitchen, doing chores, etc. are expressions of a servant's heart; and yes, this is often the case. However, what this means to many of us is that we can become really, really in love with our comfort zones.

That comfort zone is wherever you find a reason or an excuse to be busy enough to stay in the background; and frankly, it is a place that keeps you from being fully engaged with others, as was the case with Martha. There's not much love in the comfort zone because it is usually a place that is

all about "me." It's that place where you may often feel a little alone, a little put out, and a little like you're the only one
burdened about performing those background tasks that
make everything fit together. It becomes a place that keeps
you away from where you should be.

The comfort zone is also a place where we feel safe and
protected, and if we are not careful, it can become a fortress
with walls that keep others from ever finding their way
into our hearts. Maybe this was the danger that Jesus saw
in all Martha's activity—the danger of putting her chores
between her heart and His so that there was no chance of
an intimate connection. When we keep people from connecting with us, we feel we are protecting ourselves from
being hurt by others. But this is a very, very lonely life to
live. Someone needs you to be present for them, just as you
need them to be present for you. It's a risk we have to be
willing to take if we are going to love like Jesus wants us
to love. To drive home this point, 1 Peter 4:9–11 tells us to
"show hospitality to one another without grumbling. As
each as received a gift, use it to serve one another, as good
stewards of God's varied grace…as one who serves by the
strength that God supplies—in order that in everything
God may be glorified through Jesus Christ."

I get Martha. Often, I am Martha—even when I don't
want to be. I get Martha because I've also retreated behind
the walls of the kitchen, behind the scenes, to avoid hav-

ing to interact with people who might hurt me. We've all been hurt before in past relationships; this is a fact of life. But this hurt should never cause us to shut ourselves off from others.

Mary, on the other hand, acted with great discernment when she left the busyness of the kitchen and sat at Jesus's feet. She knew that hearing the heart of Christ superseded every other task that she could have been involved with at that point. She engaged her heart with His and gave Him her complete attention and worshipped Him with a heart full of pure adoration for Him. She loved Him, and she showed Him that love by listening to Him with such intensity that she was able to tune out the activity that was going on in the kitchen. Did she love her sister? Of course! But she loved Jesus more, and she recognized the value of those few moments she had with Him.

And that is the second thing I take away from this passage. Every act of service we perform must have as its ultimate motive our love for the person we are serving and our love for Christ—whether it's frying a chicken, changing a diaper, or listening as someone shares her burdens or joys. Had Martha been preparing her meal with a heart of worship and a pure love for Jesus, then her approach would have been so much different. But she saw her labors as being work that she was obligated to do because someone had to get a meal on the table. It was not an act of honor, worship, and love for the ones who would enjoy the meal but a desire to be recognized as a hardworking, successful homemaker. She let the work of her hands take her away from the feet of Jesus. As I compare these two sisters, I feel compelled to ask myself what I value the most in my life's relationships and how can I best express that. Having known so well what it's like to not feel valued, do I inadvertently make others feel that way too?

There are times when we love with an act of service, and there are times when we love by giving our undivided attention to someone. The key to knowing the difference is stopping for a moment, stepping out of our comfort zone, and really listening to the heart of the one in front of us. Love can't happen from a distance; it has to happen up close and personal. Love can't happen in a protected or a closed-up heart, a heart that only sees what I want to do for someone; it has to flow out of a heart that is yearning to know what another needs or desires. Because we have the love of Christ as one of our soul anchors, we are equipped to love others—and to love them well. The wonderful thing about it is this: because we are designed to show this kind of love to others, when we do, we are filled with a great sense of joy and fulfillment in our own lives.

Growing up in a Christian home, I experienced love every day though my parents rarely actually said the words that I recall. I didn't know that what I was experiencing was their love. I just knew that I felt safe, that I felt taken care of, that I felt a part of someone's life. Being an extremely shy person, this feeling of security was a true anchor for me; and even today, I don't ever feel a need to stray too far from wherever my home may be at any given time.

Love started to take on more nuances for me as what I call the princess fairytales began. Always a sucker for a good story, I loved hearing of Cinderella, Sleeping Beauty, and Rapunzel. Even as a small child I could somehow relate to that feeling of being mistreated and of needing to be rescued out of a dark and dreary situation (even though at that age, likely the only dark and dreary situations I faced were forced nap time, turnip greens for supper, and having to be the last one to use the bathwater on any given night).

But the connections were made. Someone who loves you will take care of you. Someone who loves you will find you beautiful. Someone who loves you will rescue you. And all that is required of you in return is that you swoon, sing, and dance in your beautiful, dainty clothes, with your beautiful dainty feet, and your beautiful, perfectly coiffed locks of pure gold (or pure ebony, depending on which princess you were). Basically, when your Prince Charming comes to rescue you, you simply pack up your adorable singing woodland creature pets, and you let yourself be rescued.

At the same time that I was growing to love these timeless fairytales, I was growing to love another story even more—the story of Jesus. Even as a child, I understood that there was a difference between the princess stories and the stories from the Bible. The stories I was taught from Scripture resonated truth within my very young soul. From the time I first heard of Him, I wanted to know this Jesus more. Even though I never felt like a princess, never looked like a princess, and never was treated like a princess, something told me I was His "princess" and that His story was meant to be a very integral part of my own life's love story.

Love manifests itself in a relationship. By definition, love requires a subject (the one who loves) and an object (the one who is loved). Because we are created in God's image, we are by nature meant to play both of these roles. We are meant to love as He loves, and we are meant to be loved. God created us to love Him and to be loved by Him, and not only did He create us to fill those roles but He also created us with the desire to fulfill them. We are to desire to be loved by Him, and we are to desire to love Him.

But we also have this innate desire to love and be loved by others, whether this love occurs within a family relationship, a friendship, or a romantic relationship. This is where it can get complicated, because we women can have those moments or life seasons when we don't feel loved at all. This may be the result of our own insecurity, or may result from how we feel we are viewed by others, or perhaps it may result from the behaviors of others. Many times I've discovered this feeling of being unloved is the result of my own unrealistic expectations about what it means to be loved. I find it very important to have a biblical understanding of what it means in my life to be the recipient of biblical love, not relying on my feelings or perceptions, but leaning into my Anchor, Jesus, to show me what it means. Otherwise, in my life, I find myself responding by retreating into a self-built fortress, fearing that I will be hurt if I open myself up to other people.

This can create such an impossible struggle for us. As someone who has come through such a struggle and is now on the other side, my friend Windie understands this struggle so well:

> *It's amazing how you can go through most of your life with very few friends. I had friends in high school, but once I married my high school sweetheart, we moved away from everything and everyone I had ever known. I was so shy and unsure of myself that I had a hard time opening up to anyone and letting them into my life as a close friend. I probably made two or three true friends over the twenty-one years we spent in the Air Force. However, that changed once we moved to Warner Robins.*
>
> *We began attending a church in the area and I could feel myself opening up a little bit more, but I still didn't*

have the true friends that God gives you to lean on and depend on. However, once I started going to the church we currently and actively attend, God really did a job on my life. It started with one friend, Sherry. We started doing things together and going places together. After that, I started longing for more friends. Well, God had that taken care of too. And where did I find them? No other place than Sunday School. We started building relationships in our class, and now I have friends that are closer to me than my own family. I know they are there for me, and I can trust them with anything. The wonderful thing about it is that God built these friendships from His love for us. And now we can provide our love to others to show them what God is like.

Unfortunately, unlike Windie, rather than seeking this love and acceptance from a loving Heavenly Father and from among the fellowship of believers, many choose to seek this love from the world's substitutes. In Romans 1, Paul writes that mankind chose to replace the glory of God for an image of man, birds, and animals; they "exchanged the truth of God for a lie," the lie that it was better to love and be loved by that which is created rather than the Creator. The end result of this was man's heart became filled with a laundry list of awful things: envy, murder, strife, deceit, malice, gossip, slander, hatred of God, insolence, arrogance, boastfulness, the invention of evil things, disobedience; they are untrustworthy, unloving, unmerciful (Rom. 1:29–32). Interestingly, each of these traits is born of self-satisfaction. It is what happens to the innermost part of us when we seek love and acceptance outside of that which is good and honorable and from the Lord. This urge for self-seeking, self-satisfying love is such an evil deception used by Satan because it keeps us from recognizing real love. It leaves us feeling unlovable, and it keeps us from knowing how to express love well to others. Ultimately, living a life in which we pursue self-satisfaction will leave us feeling more and more dissatisfied and frustrated.

The bottom line for all of us is that what we are truly seeking is unconditional love. Unconditional love is love that accepts us as we are. It forgives. It shows mercy. It is gracious and kind. It is honest and generous. Unconditional love allows us to love others even when that love is not returned and even when those we show love to hurt us in return. Unconditional love flows from that place within us that is purified by the Holy Spirit of God, that place that has been redeemed by His righteousness which covers our lives. It is the result of our following the instruction of Christ to die to ourselves daily—that is, to put aside our own needs, wishes, and wants for the sake of others—just like Christ did when He washed His disciples' feet and when He went to the cross. This is the kind of love the world needs to see in God's people. We must ruthlessly and relentlessly show unconditional, Christ-like and Spirit-initiated love to the world around us. We must relentlessly shower our brothers and sisters in Christ with this same love because without it none of us would be able to stand against the opposition that is thrown at us every day. Every single relationship we have—our marriages, our friendships, our acquaintances, our families—must overflow with this unconditional love.

Though it may sound simplistic, I can personally testify to the fact that showing that kind of love is not in the least bit simple! Loving others is hard. Life makes us tired. People make us tired. People irritate us. They hurt us and embarrass us and frustrate us. We make mistakes and do and say stupid things. We react with impatience to others and to our circumstances. However, my friends, practice does make perfect; the more we practice Christ-like love, the more easily it will start to flow from us. In *Mere Christianity*, C. S. Lewis wrote, "Do not waste time bothering whether you 'love' your neighbor; act as if you did. As soon as we do this we find one of the great secrets. When you are behaving as if you loved someone, you will presently come to love him." Furthermore, and this is very good news to me, this kind of love is not something that I have to generate; it's a fruit of the Holy Spirit that dwells within me. All I have to do is express that which He has given me the ability to express.

How do we do it? The best picture of what this kind of love looks like is in 1 Corinthians 13. It's a familiar passage for many of us, but if you're like me, you kind of get hung up on that first defining term: "patient." How can I be patient? By forgetting about myself long enough to think of the other person. Let me ask you a question. When you start to pull into a parking space at the grocery store only to discover that someone has left a shopping cart in the middle of that spot, how do you respond on your worst day? Little things like this are opportunities to practice patience. It's just a shopping cart, so you're not going to hurt anyone's feelings if you, ahem, accidentally tap it with your car or kick it with your foot between two other cars instead of taking it to the cart return. It may sound odd, but practicing patience with inanimate objects can be a good way to prepare for the patience you're going to need with the people in the store or at your house.

Assuming we have the patience thing covered, what else does love look like? Paul says that love is also kind; it isn't jealous or boastful or arrogant. It doesn't act unbecomingly or rudely; it does not seek its own. It isn't provoked and doesn't take into account a wrong it has suffered. It doesn't rejoice in unrighteousness but rejoices with the truth. It bears all things, believes all things, hopes all things, and endures all things (vs. 4–7). Sometimes as I read this list, I kind of get the idea that maybe Paul understood love in this way because he understood all too well how it felt to be hated and despised. Other times, I think of what the Corinthians must have thought when they read this. They had such a worldly view of what love was—much like what our world's philosophy teaches today. To read that love has such pure virtues tied to it must have been a very powerful experience for them, and one which likely opened their eyes to an entirely new way to look at life. I can't help but imagine how Paul's teaching on love changed the lives of these believers.

One thing I find so compelling about the virtues of love is that each one of them comes from an act of will. These virtues are not undisciplined reactions to circumstances; they are not emotional outcries. They are simply choices made over the course of our days spent with others. People who are patient don't have some special, mystical skill. They choose to be patient even when it is difficult to be. Kindness is also a choice as is treating others with courtesy and choosing not to be offended when someone does something to hurt you. See, in this passage, Paul isn't just describing the way we act toward our spouses, our families, or our friends. He is painting a picture of what the fullness of our lives will look like when we make the choice to act in loving ways. I don't know about you, but that is exactly how I want the portrait of my life to look.

Recently, one very rainy day, the Lord gave me a couple of object lessons to show me that whether or not I respond in His love toward others is all about my choice. The rain was really pouring on this particular evening when I pulled up outside of the gym for my workout. A lady who was parked in the first space on the street right in front of me dashed out of the building and got into her car. I waited so I could pull up and free more parking space; it's all parallel parking there, and this is what the gym patrons usually do whenever possible to keep anyone from having to back into that first space. So I waited for her to move, but she didn't, except to look in her rearview mirror at me. Finally, after waiting about five minutes, I grabbed my stuff and made a mad dash for the door. Just as I opened my car door to the deluge, she drove away. Now I'm not saying she sat there and waited for me to get out of the car, but it sure was mighty suspicious.

After the gym, I had to go to the gas station. I was almost on empty and didn't want to risk trying to go before work the following day or I never would have gone in such terrible weather. The driver in the vehicle in front of me had pulled up to the pump and stopped and turned off his vehicle. The only problem was that he actually was in that no man's land between pumps. This meant that I had to pull in pretty close to his car just so that the nozzle would reach my gas tank. And then I had to stand in the blowing rain, counting the seconds between thunder and lightning, while I pumped my gas. No one ever got out of that vehicle in front of me, even though I could clearly see four people moving around. I guess they were going to wait out the rain. Maybe they're still there.

I share these little incidents to show how easy it is for us to lose patience with others when our convenience is compromised or when we feel that someone has slighted us. Because I did, I confess, begin to feel impatient. However, this is not the way I think that I, as a Christ-follower, should react.

I am called to a higher standard; I am called to die to self daily so my own rights and preferences are no longer an issue. I am called to replace impatience with long-suffering and mercy—to overlook the slights and offenses others make against me and to look for ways that I can fill my heart with compassion for them. It is often the people who need mercy, compassion, forgiveness, and grace the most are those who, in our eyes, deserve it the least. And this is where I have to humbly confess that I stand among those least deserving.

It is remembering this truth—the truth that I don't deserve the forgiveness and the patience of others—that helps me to curb that tendency to get frustrated or impatient, to make that heavy sigh sound that equates to an audible version of a pout. Perhaps it goes against society's norms to admit our flaws or weaknesses. But when we do, boy, does it change our perspective on others. We stop waiting for others to start treating us fairly. We begin to realize that Jesus's golden rule begins with a command to His children to treat others well—the way that we ourselves want to be treated. And by the way, does it strike anyone else as interesting that the "golden rule" is not a "golden promise"? The passage doesn't say that others will treat us well if we treat them well. It just says that's the way we're supposed to live, no matter how others choose to treat us in return.

I want to be kinder to people, not just in my words and actions but in such a way that the kindness of my words and actions are an overflow of a heart filled with kindness toward them, no matter what. I'm reminded of one of my favorite quotes by missionary Amy Carmichael. She wrote, "A cup brimful of sweet water cannot spill even one drop of bitter water, no matter how suddenly jolted." That sweet water comes from the love of God being poured out in my heart.

Back in 1 Corinthians 13, Paul goes on to say in this great "love chapter" of the Bible that though every other gift will pass away, love never fails. The apostle ends this chapter with this verse: "But now faith, hope, love, abide these three; but the greatest of these is love." Have you ever wondered why Paul rates love above faith and hope? It is because, I believe, that our faith and our hope will one day be realized when we finally see Jesus face to face. In Heaven, there will be no more need for faith and hope because every object of our faith will be within sight. But love is that one virtue that will anchor us for all eternity.

I wanted to end this chapter with one woman's love story that didn't quite turn out the way that she had hoped or that she would have ever expected, but her story did not come as a surprise to her Heavenly Father. In fact, the Lord is using her story to provide deep encouragement and ministry to other women in similar circumstances. I think many of us never realize the depth and breadth of all the ways God loves us until we are left feeling very unloved. Here is Sonya's story:

> *I was so surprised when Chrissie asked me to share my story in the area of love. I was thinking, Why would she ask me? I have a failed marriage. That is how good I am in the area of love. I was thinking she should ask someone who has celebrated their fiftieth wedding anniversary if she wants a story about love, but I decided to share my experiences.*
>
> *I had been married for twenty-seven years. I married my high school sweetheart. He was the only man I had ever loved in the romantic kind of love. One night, my husband said to me, "I am not in love with you anymore." I cannot put into words how I felt for the next months and even years to come over that one sentence. I felt like I was in the commercial where the elephant*

sits on people's chest. I felt like I couldn't breathe. I have always believed love is a choice we make every day and is not a feeling that comes and goes. Shortly after that, he said he wanted a divorce. I never knew until this time how devastating divorce was to so many people I knew.

As time went on, I realized that although my husband did not love me anymore, there were so many other people who did. The most important realization was that God loved me. God's love was unconditional. I had never experienced God's love so deeply before. Honestly, I had never needed God's love so desperately before. My husband had always been there to take care of me, to provide for me, to be my security, to be my protector, and to be the one I shared everything with. Now my husband was gone, and I was alone. I learned to trust God to be all of those things for me. God provided for me in so many ways, and it was amazing to experience His love. God not only has met my needs but also has given me some of the desires of my heart.

Another way I have experienced love on a higher and deeper level is from my family and friends. I always knew my daughters loved me, but I did not realize how much until after my divorce. They were there for me in every way. They both make more money than I do, and they have offered to pay for my car repairs or other financial responsibilities that would come up.

Thankfully, I never had to take money from them, but it was so comforting to know that they were willing to give it. My daughters also made sure I wasn't alone when I had surgery or medical procedures done. They have been there to take good care of me. God truly blessed me with two wonderful daughters!

The last area in which I have experienced love was with my friends and church family. They were and still are here for me. They listened to me, called me, visited me, cried with me, and prayed with me and for me. The Lord has provided an opportunity for me to love people who are going through separation and divorce. I never knew this ministry existed before my divorce.

I am very thankful and blessed to have so much love in my life!

Learn It and Live It: Anchored by Love

Have you ever felt invisible? Explain.

_____

_____

_____

_____

_____

What do you think it means to experience true love?

_____

_____

_____

_____

_____

Read John 13:3–5 and summarize the passage below.

_____

_____

_____

_____

_____

Verse 3 says that Jesus "knew" something. What was it? Why does this fact make the act He performed in washing the disciples' feet even more profound? What does this teach you about yourself? About love?

_____

_____

_____

_____

_____

Read Philippians 2:6–8 and summarize the description given of Christ.

_____

_____

_____

_____

_____

Next, read Philippians 2:5–8. How does adding verse 5 change your perspective on the attitude we should have toward others in order to be able to express our love to them?

_____

_____

_____

_____

_____

Read John 13:12-15. What was Jesus's purpose of washing the disciples' feet?

_____

_____

_____

_____

_____

Read Luke 10:38-42. With which of the sisters do you most identify, and why? Which sister did Jesus say had the right idea on that day? Why? What does this tell you about how we express love to others?

_____

_____

_____

_____

_____

What was the difference in the two sisters' attitudes?

_____

_____

_____

_____

_____

What is your definition of "comfort zone?" Do you have one? What is it, and what does it mean to you?

_____

_____

_____

_____

_____

Name a time when someone made you feel loved and valued. How did you respond?

_____

_____

_____

_____

_____

How do we know how best to express our love to others?

_____

_____

_____

_____

_____

Think back to various times in your life when you began to understand what love means. Tell about some of those times, whether good or bad, right or wrong.

_____

_____

_____

_____

_____

Think back to various times in your life when you felt that you expressed true, unconditional love for someone.

_____

_____

_____

_____

_____

Read Romans 1:29–32. What are some substitutes the world has used for love? What does this passage say was the effect these substitutes have had on man's heart?

_____

_____

_____

_____

_____

How would you define unconditional love?

_____

_____

_____

_____

_____

Read 1 Corinthians 13. List the characteristics of love and give a definition for each one.

_____

_____

_____

_____

_____

How does our natural tendency to seek our own welfare and comfort compete with our desire to love and be loved?

_____

_____

_____

_____

_____

Think of someone that you find difficult to love. How could you express your love to that person?

_____

_____

_____

_____

_____

Anchored by Truth

FOR THE MANY years I have been preparing and teaching Bible studies—whether for children or adults—what I have come to realize is that many people apparently have Bibles that take on an unbearable weight during the week, such that it is impossible to pick them up. Some Bibles actually disappear entirely during the week. When church time comes around, their Bibles have magically transformed back to their normal condition. Have you ever experienced this phenomenon at your house?

All joking aside, it is quite sad how many American Christians neglect God's Word except on Sundays. Of all the anchors that we are considering here, the anchor of truth is the anchor that defines all the other anchors of love, peace, and freedom. In fact, without the anchor of truth, none of the others would exist. God's Word anchors us to Him and is what directs us to fulfill our purpose in life. The Westminster Catechism, which is a declaration of the biblical beliefs of Protestant churches, begins with the following two questions/answers:

Q1. What is the chief end of man? The chief end of man is to glorify God and to enjoy Him forever.

Q2. What rule hath God given to direct us how we may glorify and enjoy Him? The Word of God…is the only rule to direct us how we may glorify and enjoy Him.

God's truth, His Word, anchors us in every aspect of our lives. It is our guide for our relationship with Him and with others. It teaches us how to manage our money. It teaches us how to respond to life's difficulties. It teaches us how to live pleasing lives before God. It reminds us in our worst times of His everlasting love for us, of His forgiveness, and of His redemption. It teaches us about eternity and encourages us that our home is with Him. God's Word teaches us how to be a good spouse, a good parent, a good worker, a good friend. It is a road map showing us the way to Heaven. It is a guide book, a history book, a love story.

Though so many American Christians neglect their Bibles, there are Christians all over the world who would give anything to have one. Men and women risk their lives every day to smuggle Bibles into hostile and restricted areas of the world, where owning a copy of the Bible may cost them their lives. Still, they long for God's Word. They long for that overwhelming sense of fellowship with the Lord that comes every time the Bible is opened. The Bible is the source of their hope, and despite the danger owning one holds for them, they would give anything to hold that hope in their hands. To open it and draw the pages to their faces, inhaling the fragrance of ink and paper, which is to them the fragrance of life. And yet, in our homes and even in our churches, multiple copies sit undisturbed on shelves, under car seats, or on tables where they're used as coasters. Maybe it is time that we all renew our love for God's Word.

In Scripture, the first time man encountered God's written Word was when God gave the Ten Commandments to Moses. Prior to that time, God spoke directly to His people, whether in person, like Adam and Eve, Abraham, Jacob, etc., or through one of His prophets, like Moses. Though many see the commandments as just a list of impossible rules that God arbitrarily instituted reminding us of how incapable we are of following them, I see these commands as a sign of mercy from a gracious God. God wants us to know Him and to know His expectations for us. Having God's commands, precepts, and expectations in written form indicates His great desire to communicate to us how we can be in a relationship with Him. We can return to His Word time after time to gain new understanding about who He is and who He has designed us to be. Each time we open His Word, we are experiencing sweet fellowship with Him. In giving us His Word, He has given us access to His heart. What a powerful act of mercy, grace, and love this is.

To understand this better, let's recall the circumstances that surrounded God's first giving His Word to His people.

The Israelites had gone into Egypt during the time of Joseph in order to escape a great famine. At the time, Joseph and the Hebrews were in good favor with the Egyptians despite the fact that the Israelites worshiped the one true God and the Egyptians worshiped many gods. Over the next three hundred to four hundred years, the Israelites grew in number; and it seems the longer they remained in Egypt, the more they were likely influenced by the polytheistic philosophies that were practiced among the Egyptians, even incorporating some of those practices and philosophies into their own worship.

When they were finally freed from Egyptian slavery and on their way into the wilderness, the Lord continued to hear their grumbling; and for every complaint, He had a provision. But the provision came in His time and through His conditions. Here's an example in Exodus 15:22–27. The Israelites were three days in the wilderness and had found no water. Then when they did come upon a place where water was available, it was not drinkable. I find this significant because the people were very clearly being led by God on their way; chapter 13 of Exodus describes the pillar of fire by night and the pillar of cloud by day that showed them the way—a visible representation of God's physical presence with them. Why, then, did God allow them to get thirsty? At Marah, according to verse 25, the Lord instructed Moses to throw a tree in the water to make it sweet; and the people drank. At that point, the Bible says the Lord used this situation as an opportunity to instruct them. Verse 25b–27 says "there He made for them a statute and regulation, and there He tested them. And He said, 'If you will give earnest heed to the voice of the Lord your God, and do what is right in His sight, and give ear to His commandments, and keep all His statutes, I will put none of the diseases on you which I have put on the Egyptians; for I the Lord am your healer.' Then they came to Elim where there were twelve springs of water and seventy date palms, and they camped there beside the waters."

In these verses, God clearly tells the Israelites that it is necessary for them to obey His commands. This shows us that even before Moses brought those God-inscribed tablets down from the mountain, God was giving them instruction. He was letting them know how He expected them to live. But for the Hebrews and for us, He knew there was something about the written Word that would allow them to be on the same page (sorry for the pun) about His expectations. The written Word would be a visual reminder of His commands.

In this situation in the desert, the Lord showed His people that obedience to His truth would yield a blessing. By depriving them of water, He showed them their need to cling to Him; He showed Himself to be their Provider, Healer, Protector, and Anchor. As time went on and the Israelites continued to face hardship in the wilderness, they continued to question and complain; but God continued to take care of them, and He continued to remind them that the way they would identify themselves as His was through obedience to Him. I have to think this must have gotten pretty tedious for Him. Have you ever worked really hard to take care of someone who could only find fault with your efforts? Either you didn't act quickly enough or maybe you did things your own way instead of the way "Mother" would have done it. Whatever the case may have been, we all know it's never fun being around someone who complains all the time!

The Lord had great mercy on His people because He remembered what they had been through and He remembered His covenant with them. Despite their negativism and murmuring, the Lord continued to desire a relationship with them. His words in Exodus 19:4 are such an expression of love and desire from God for His people. He says, "You yourselves have seen what I did to the Egyptians, and how I bore you on eagles' wings and brought you to Myself. Now then, if you will indeed obey My voice and keep My covenant, then you shall be My own possession among all the peoples, for all the earth is Mine; and you shall be to Me a kingdom of priests and a holy nation."

God loved them and wanted to give them all His blessings, but this was conditional upon their keeping up their side of the covenant with Him. He needed this to be a two-way relationship, and the way He desires for His people to show their love for Him is through obedience. For the Israelites, He spelled it out—how their obedience needed to look. So He had Moses and the leaders consecrate the people and prepare for Him to come down to the mountain. When it was time, God came down, and Moses went up. And while Moses was receiving God's law for His people, the Israelites grew impatient, and they went right back to what they knew in Egypt.

In Exodus 19:8, 24:3, and 24:7, the people had made a commitment: "All the people answered, 'All the words which the Lord has spoken, we will do!'" Three times the people pledged their obedience to the Lord. Three times, the Lord warned them about making a false idol from gold or silver. And then, when Moses tarried on the mountain, what is it that they did?

While Moses was on the mountain, the Israelites had Aaron craft a golden calf for them to bow down to—an idol that they believed would lead them forward and be their god. This was the only understanding they had, the only way they knew to get themselves out of the situation they felt they were in. They had given Moses a try, but by all appearances, Moses had gotten killed in the thunder and lightning going up on that mountain he had climbed. They were ready to move on, and the only way they knew to go was backward.

But God in His mercy and grace, knowing what His people were doing in the camp, continued on, dictating His law to Moses so that His people would understand Him and how they should live in relationship with Him and with one another. As the people were at the foot of the mountain, forming a false god to worship and follow, the God who wants them to know Him and love Him and who wants to bless them, began His instructions to them by reminding them who He is: "I am the Lord your God, who brought you out of the land of Egypt, out of the house of slavery. You shall have no other gods before Me" (Exod. 20:2–3). They knew this already, but in their circumstances, they had forgotten. Despite this, God continued to take His time, giving the people every opportunity to come to their senses and stop the process of god-making. Sadly, they did not nor did their leaders point them in the right direction.

Upon reading Exodus 32, we now discover there are some pretty harsh consequences for the people who committed the idolatry without repenting. What about you? Have you ever failed to keep a commitment to obey the Lord's commands? Did you experience consequences? How did God use His Word to draw you back to Him and to comfort you? Elizabeth tells her very candid story about how God's Word impacted her in a season of her life where things had gotten terribly offtrack:

> *It's easy to live for Jesus, to say "I'll follow and obey You" when life is calm, unchallenging, and going my way. Smooth sailing. Life was just dandy. I had set up my life exactly the way I wanted it and was living a godly life and had godly plans for it! Then one morning I woke up to life stabbing me in the heart with the knife of adultery. My spirituality didn't hold me up; I crumbled.*
>
> *Voices devoid of God's, personal opinions, and my own raw emotions blew me toward the rocks of my own destruction. My smooth sailing turned into a tempest tossed; and I found, too late, that I wasn't anchored like I thought. Soon I couldn't think of anything but escape. My bags packed, God stopped me at the door and challenged me to now practice what I had been preaching: James 1:22. He reminded me that on my wedding day I had made vows to Him as well as to my husband: Psalm 56:12. And He reminded me of His promises of blessing to the obedient, as in Deuteronomy 28. So with a huff and a "Fine!" I locked myself in my room and chose to cast my anchor in His Word.*
>
> *I didn't know where to start, but God was faithful to point out Scriptures I needed while reading. Suddenly, verses I knew my whole life seemed to leap off the pages*

and become real. God was showing me His Truth, and I couldn't drink it in fast enough; they were life when I felt like I was dying. His words were contrary to the words of others, yet they were the ones that held me firm and gave me hope. They gave me the confidence, the courage, and the strength to stay where I was. They gave me a game plan. In the book of Hosea, He convicted me of having been unfaithful to God, yet He redeemed me anyway! My verse for application was 1 Peter 2:21–25: Be like Christ, who forgives and redeems. Ephesians 4:29–32 was my obedience challenge, and boy, was it challenging! Exodus 14:13–14 was God's promise to me. He would do the real work.

This is how important God's Word is to Him, and it shows why it should be of utmost priority in our lives as well. He wants us to know Him. He wants us to focus our hearts, our souls, and our might on loving Him (Deut. 6:5). When knowing and loving God is our life's pursuit, then everything we experience in this life—joys, sorrows, or even the mundane—will be informed by the overwhelming love and grace He brings into our lives. One of the most significant places we find those expressions of love and begin to understand the expressions of His grace is in His Word.

Feeling loved and lavished with grace sounds wonderful, doesn't it? Yet even though so many of us long for this, so few of us are willing or feel able to spend the time and effort it takes to really wait on God, His Word open before us. The psalmist wrote of his own desire to hear from God: "My soul is crushed with longing after your ordinances at all times…My soul languishes for Your salvation; I wait for Your Word. My eyes fail with longing for Your Word" (Ps. 119:20, 81–82). Have we ever experienced such love for God that we languished for His Word? I don't know about you, but that is not an everyday occurrence for me. But I want it to be. Robyn shares her story of how God's Word has been her anchor throughout her life and how the Lord has used His Word to encourage her, affirm her, and love her.

As a young child, I learned from my parents and Sunday School teachers that Scripture was true and trustworthy. I never doubted that truth even as I grew in head knowledge and increasing heart knowledge. But then life happened, and the truth I understood became my anchor in the calm and storms of daily life. Philippians 4:13 was my verse: "I can do all things through Christ who strengthens me."

One of the biggest storms I have ever faced came when I was twenty-six years old; I was a wife and a mom, and I was pregnant with my second child. One December night, the phone rang with news that my father had committed suicide. I was stunned and angry because this was not who he was. I knew his testimony and that he was saved. I could not understand why. The Word became my stronghold and anchor that night like never before. After thirty years, it still is.

There have been other times of storms: my mom's walk with cancer and her death, church ministry stresses with my pastor husband, my journey with depression and the life-threatening complications when my precious granddaughter was born. I sat in the chapel at the hospital that day for hours reading Scripture and begging God to spare her life. My new life verse was my strength. Jeremiah 29:11 says, "I know the plans I have for you." I held on to that promise and many more in the days ahead. Yes, He not only spared her life but has also made her completely whole and healthy. Then and today, Christ is my Anchor. His Word is still my strength and stronghold. I trust Him because Scripture tells me so.

There's another aspect of our being anchored in God's truth: not only must we hear it, read it, learn it, and believe it but we must also obey it. James writes, "For if anyone is a hearer of the word and not a doer, he is like a man who looks at his natural face in a mirror; for once he has looked at himself and gone away, he has immediately forgotten what kind of person he was. But one who looks intently at the perfect law, the law of liberty, and abides by it, not having become a forgetful hearer but an effectual doer, this man will be blessed in what he does" (James 1:23–25).

Back in Psalm 119, we read that there is a process to this thing. The psalmist writes, "I will meditate on Your precepts and regard Your ways. I shall delight in Your statutes; I shall not forget Your Word" (Ps. 119:15–16). In both of these passages, we learn that as we read God's Word, we are to do so with intention. That means we don't just read it as a feel-good, warm, and fuzzy way to start our day in a good mood. It means we read it with the intention of doing what it says. When the Word says to repent, we will repent. When the Word says to love, we will love. When the Word says to worship, we will worship. When the Word says to obey, we will obey.

To be able to obey God's Word means we have to read it intently—that is, with determination. The passage in James 1 always resonates with me. That picture of looking in a mirror then walking away and forgetting what I just saw reminds me so much of myself. I can let so many things keep me from remembering, and acting, on what I've seen.

For example, the windshield on my car is very dirty. But the only time I really think about how dirty my windshield is, is when the sun is shining on it. You know, when I'm traveling east in the morning on the way to work or west in the evenings on the way home from work. Those are the times when I can't really see too well out the windshield, and I think to myself, "I should really clean this!" But I get home and never think of my dirty windshield again until the following morning when the sun is shining, and I can't see where I'm going.

Forgetting what God's Word says about me is a much bigger deal though. I don't want to be the person who is careless with my soul. God's Word is all I have to depend on in this world to tell me how to be something other than this person who walks around thinking that she is one thing when really she is something else entirely. This, my friend, is a very foolish person. James writes, "But one who looks intently at the perfect law, the law of liberty, and abides by it, not having become a forgetful hearer but an effectual doer, this man will be blessed in what he does."

Two things I definitely want to be: *effective* and *blessed*. And these two things go hand in hand. This is a person who looks intently—that is, with intention to understand God's Word and its relevance to every aspect of life. This is a person who goes beyond good intentions to having a deep respect for God's perfect, liberating law, a respect that leads to effective obedience. It leads to life change and heart change. Looking intently requires us to live carefully and with great deliberation in this world. It requires that we act on God's instruction and not react out of our emotions or distorted understanding of our circumstances. It leads to our handling our souls and the souls of others with great tenderness and mercy and grace.

Sometimes we forget what we saw in the mirror because we don't like what we see. Sometimes we just don't care to look deeply because we don't want to face what's below the surface. Always, it is easier to draw attention to the faults and blemishes of others rather than to tend to our own faults and blemishes. However, God's Word offers liberty, fulfillment, and blessings when we live by it. I want that. All of it.

The remarkable thing about God's Word is this: when we begin to invest our time into reading and obeying and into listening for His voice, we will begin to feel that strong connection with Him. Like the Israelites, He will bring us to Himself. The more time we begin to spend in His presence, the harder it will become to leave.

In Jesus's prayer in the Garden of Gethsemane, recorded in John 17, He asks His Father to sanctify His followers in the truth and gives testimony to the fact that God's Word is truth (John 17:17). John MacArthur explains this verse means that as believers, we are set apart for God and His purposes alone. We are to do only what God wants, and we are to hate all that God hates. In this way, we become coworkers with Jesus to accomplish God's will in this world.

You know who really, really hates that? Satan does. And he will do all he can do to keep us from experiencing the power available to us in God's Word.

Unfortunately, he doesn't have too hard of a job in most cases. Too many of us don't give too much effort when it comes to the day-to-day immersion into His Word. Oh, I don't say this to be judgmental; I'm just stating a fact—of which I am guilty most days myself. I let the distractions of this life crowd out my time with the Lord on more days than I'd like to admit, using all sorts of excuses. Interruptions like a buzzing phone, an incoming text message, or the timer on the dryer (although I can usually let that one go) all serve as my reasons for getting offtrack when it's time to sit down with my Bible. Essentially, when I bring my phone with me to Bible study, what I'm saying to myself is that I don't want to miss a call or a message from a friend or work or whoever, but I'm okay with missing the message the Lord might have for me. Ouch! Yes, that one really hurt. It tells the Lord what my priorities are, and frankly, it isn't the friends or whoever wants to reach me. It's myself—look how important I am that I must be reachable at all times. (Wow, just writing this makes me long for life before cell phones!) Satan doesn't even have to try with those of us who won't put our phones down.

Satan does not want us to be equipped with the power offered through God's Word. He doesn't want us to be aligned with advancing God's Kingdom in this earth. He doesn't want us to change and grow closer to God. He will make sure that any obstacle he can throw in our path hits its target. We must be prepared for this!

When it comes to your personal time of Bible study, what is your plan? Do you have one of those devotional magazines you pick up from the church that offers a little story and a Bible verse? Do you take sermon notes at church and use those for deeper study during the week? Do you have a one-year Bible or a Bible reading app that you use? Do you have a plan?

Going back to the verses in Psalm 119:15–16, we see a pretty decent plan of action when it comes to effectively absorbing God's Word. First, the psalmist says he meditates on God's precepts. The term "meditate" here literally means to "repeat aloud to oneself." In my mind, I picture a student reciting his spelling words over and over, his mouth moving to form every letter, until he can spell the words without error. In this verse, the psalmist is talking about really trying to understand on a cognitive level what God's Word is saying. Too often when reading the Bible, I find myself just skimming through until I get to whatever I think the point is. I don't savor every word and every thought on the page, saying the words over and over to myself. But here we see that knowing and understanding is the important first step.

Next, he "regards" or gives respect to God's ways. He pays attention to what he is learning about God. In other words, he applies what he is learning about God. *Regard* shows that he is determined to be obedient, that he recognizes the applicability of God's truth to his own life.

Third, he says he delights in God's statutes. This delight, or joy, may not happen immediately. But as we begin to obey and apply the Word of God, we begin to see our lives change. We feel the results of drawing closer to God, and this brings us joy. Finally, he says that he shall not forget God's Word. This is quite important to the process because the change the Lord wants to make in us is not temporary. It is lifelong. It is eternal. How many times have we heard those age-old crisis promises like "If you only get me out of this, then I will…" Fill in the blank with whatever promise you think will appeal to God in that particular moment. The psalmist is saying here that the change he is making in his life is not a temporary thing but it is a change to his very being as a person. God is changing who he is, and therefore, he cannot forget the Lord's Word. Not only that but God has also promised blessings to the one who hears and obeys His Word, so the psalmist is not likely to forget the blessings that are tied to God's Word.

Closely tied to the study of God's Word is the discipline of effective prayer. Throughout Psalm 119, the psalmist offers prayers for understanding, prayers for blessing, and prayers of commitment. Tying prayer to Bible study allows us to humble our hearts and hear more deeply what the Lord is saying to us. Praying involves intimacy with

God and waiting for Him to speak to us. It requires us to place our hearts and our minds in the right posture of reverence and dependence on Him so that He can fellowship with us. This is the kind of relationship He desires for us to have with Him. Prayer puts us in a posture to acknowledge the Word we are studying truly is the Word of God and without the discernment His Holy Spirit gives us, we cannot fully understand His Word. Finally, prayer allows us to know Him more deeply and discern His Word from all the other voices that we hear in our world.

Discernment in these days is critical to our holding firm to the anchor of God's truth. In 2 Timothy, Paul warns about the false teachers who hold to a form of godliness that lacks power because it twists the Word of God into a different message. He warns, "For among them are those who enter into households and captivate weak women weighted down with sins, led on by various impulses, always learning and never able to come to the knowledge of the truth."

Here's what was happening then and what is still happening today: false teachers knew just enough about the Bible that they could turn the Scriptures into a feel-good message, a message that made sin acceptable, ignoring the message of repentance and holiness. These false teachers preyed upon women who were weighed down with emotional and spiritual guilt over their sins; and though they were always trying to find some system of belief that would save them, for whatever reason, they never landed on the true Gospel with the power to truly save. In our time, when there is such a focus on the religion of "me," it is more important than ever to live with the discernment that comes from relying on the Holy Spirit informing our hearts and minds through the Word of God. We have to be faithful to compare every religious book we read, every sermon we hear, or every Bible lesson we are taught to the truth of God's Word. We must be so careful not to buy into Facebook theology (those pithy quotes with pretty pictures that sound so good but are deceptively superficial) or Christian radio theology that can really play on our emotions. Spiritual discernment, however, only comes as we immerse ourselves in the study of God's Word on a daily basis. We can't recognize what is false until we know how to recognize God's Truth.

Like all the other anchors we have discussed, the anchor of God's truth involves a choice, a determined and disciplined act of the will that overcomes our natural tendencies. However, like all these anchors, these choices can sometimes be difficult to make, no matter how strong our desire. I am convinced, however, that if we can develop a lifestyle of deep and consistent fellowship with God, we can strengthen our hold on all the other anchors. Let's look at a few ways we can make the time we spend in God's Word more valuable.

First, find the best time of day to be free of other distractions and obligations. I am decidedly not a morning person. It takes me a good long cup of coffee before I am awake enough to have a coherent thought. But I have discovered that early morning is the most quiet time of my day. My mind is not cluttered with things I need to do, and I don't have to worry about the phone ringing or anyone stopping by. When I first decided to have my Bible and prayer time in the morning, it was a chore; but now I wake up looking forward to it (and that first cup of coffee). Morning may not be your best time. The point is to identify the time of day when you are most available to hear God's voice and commit that time every day to fellowship with Him.

Second, have a plan. There are many good Bible reading plans and apps available these days. You may have to try a few out before you find one you can commit to. Having a reading plan helps you to be consistent, and it helps you to build your knowledge of God's Word systematically instead of randomly. There are also podcasts and online resources of daily Bible teachings that may help keep you focused and are good for those who may find it easier to follow a teacher. Often, during what I call "knitting season," I will plug in my earbuds and listen to podcasts of Bible teachers I trust while I get in a few extra minutes of knitting time. As helpful as this can be, it is important to note that listening must be in addition to reading. It's important that we spend ample time reading God's Word for ourselves rather than always merely listening to what someone else has to say about God's Word.

Third, use a journal. You don't have to use something fancy; just a plain spiral notebook will do. I use one journal for my quiet time, another one for my actual journal, and a third spiral notebook for sermon notes. Okay, so maybe this is excessive. But what can I say? I have always loved having stuff to write on. Anyway, using a journal will help you to focus your thoughts, record verses that stand out to you, and list points of prayer that come to your mind as you read.

A word of warning about some of the teaching that goes around periodically about journaling: there are some who advocate a method of journaling in which you write without thinking about what you're writing—that you simply clear your mind and write whatever words come to you. This is actually a very dangerous occult practice known as *automatic writing* and should be avoided.

Fourth, make yourself accountable to someone. I recommend that every Christian woman have a prayer and accountability partner who is not a spouse. This kind of accountability is a wonderful growth experience. Your accountability and prayer partner is someone you can be completely transparent with, someone with whom you can share the best and the worst of yourself with, someone who will encourage you and instruct you in God's Word. Choose this person wisely. I always prefer to find someone who is older in the Lord than I am, who understands the particular life challenges that I face. Pray about making this commitment to accountability in your life and see who the Lord sends your way. It can be such a wonderful source of encouragement as you grow in your faith.

Finally, commit to change. Remember that growing in the knowledge of God's truth is not just a good pastime; it is meant to draw us closer to Him and make us more like Christ. Make a daily commitment to change the things that He shows you. In your journal, list those things that God is asking you to confess and to repent of, the people you need to forgive, and the habits you need to change. Then make it a point to revisit those things on a daily basis to track your progress. You will be encouraged as you see yourself being changed according to His Word.

Our job in God's Kingdom is to submit to the change He wants to make in our hearts on a daily basis and to understand that as He changes us from moment to moment, He is making us more in the image of Christ (Rom. 8:28–30), with the end result of filling our hearts with complete joy (1 John 1:4). This eternal work is what every believer's longing should be.

As I've been sitting in my chair writing this chapter, my sweet rescue cat has made multiple attempts to get in my lap. He crosses over two pieces of furniture, tries to reach out to push my MacBook out of his way, makes his disappointed sound, then treks back over to his spot in the window when he realizes that it's not yet "lap time." His joy is my warm lap—being close to the one who rescued him from a bad situation, who takes care of him, and who loves him.

Our joy comes from being close to our Father—drawing closer to Him with every opportunity we are given. The great thing about that is, we never have to compete with anything else He is doing at the moment. He keeps that spot closest to His heart open for us. No matter the circumstances we may find ourselves in this world, close to Him is where our joy and our peace will be found. It takes just a moment to make the choice to be there in that place where His light warms our lives, burning through the coldness the dark has left in us. This happens each time we open His Word and enter His presence through prayer. It is through His Word that we are completely exposed to the kindness and love He has for us. It is through His Word that He offers us forgiveness, unconditional love and acceptance, Himself, and His righteousness.

Learn It and Live It: Anchored by Truth

What are your habits when it comes to your Bible? Do you reach for it once a day or more? Once each week? Are you satisfied with your commitment to reading and studying God's Word daily?

_____

_____

_____

_____

_____

List at least three life changes that you have addressed over the past month as a direct result of your personal Bible study.

Take a moment and reflect on this statement: "God's truth, His Word, anchors us in every aspect of our lives." Respond to that by thinking of at least three ways this statement is true in your life.

1. _____
   _____
   _____
   _____
   _____

2. _____
   _____
   _____
   _____
   _____

3. _____
   _____
   _____
   _____
   _____

Do you ever take God's Word for granted? Take a few moments to read or listen to some of the testimonies on *namepeoples.imb.org* or *persecution.com* to find out how you can minister to people who could be killed or imprisoned if caught with a Bible. Does this change your perspective on how to be a better steward of your Bible?

_____

_____

_____

_____

_____

Read Exodus 19:9–25. This is the scene leading up to God's giving Moses the Ten Commandments. In your own words, describe the scene, listing the details you find significant. Use the following questions to help you.

1. Who was allowed to go up the mountain?

_____

_____

_____

_____

_____

2. What happened if someone touched the mountain
   while God's presence was there?

   _____

   _____

   _____

   _____

   _____

3. Who did God request Moses bring with him?

   _____

   _____

   _____

   _____

   _____

4. Now read Hebrews 12:18–29. What are the differences between Mount Sinai and Mount Zion? What do you think is the primary difference between the two experiences?

_____

_____

_____

_____

_____

Read Exodus 20:18–26. God had several requirements/ expectations He gave His people. Read these below and give the verse reference where these requirements are found.

1. That reverence for Him would keep His people from sin. Verse _____
2. That His people should not make other gods to serve. Verse _____
3. That they should make an altar and give sacrifices to Him on it. Verse _____

4. That they must not use tools to cut stones for the altar. Verse _____ (This ensured that the carvers were not tempted to carve the stone into an idol.)

5. That steps not be a part of the altar so as not to expose their nakedness. Verse _____

Read Exodus 19:8, 24:3, and 24:7. What was the commitment that the Israelites made? Do you think they were sincere?

_____

_____

_____

_____

_____

Now read Exodus 32 and describe what happens. As you read, make note of the progression of the events. What does this tell you about our tendency to say one thing but do the opposite? Have you ever done this? What were the consequences for the people's idolatry? What were the consequences for your disobedience?

_____

_____

_____

_____

_____

Tell about a time you grew impatient with God and resorted to your own wisdom. What was the outcome? Was it the outcome you wanted?

_____

_____

_____

_____

_____

Read Deuteronomy 6:1–11 and fill in the answers.

1. Summarize the people's responsibility concerning God's commands.

_____

_____

_____

_____

_____

2. List the promises that God makes if His people obey
His Word.

_____

_____

_____

_____

_____

Read Psalm 119:20, 81–82. What was driving the psalmist's desire for God's Word? Dig a little deeper in the verses
of this chapter. Write down any verses that stand out to you
and explain why.

_____

_____

_____

_____

_____

James 1:23–25 speaks of being a doer of the Word. Read these verses carefully and consider areas of your life where you easily hear or read God's instruction but struggle with obeying it.

_____

_____

_____

_____

_____

What obstacles seem to consistently be in your way when it comes to time in God's Word? Write them down below with a plan of action to eliminate them.

_____

_____

_____

_____

_____

Read 2 Timothy 3:6. What are some of the worldly philosophies that we often hear being preached or taught as
Gospel but which have no power? Are there some that you
find appealing only to discover later are totally unbiblical?
When do you find yourself most susceptible to being lured
in by such teachings?

_____

_____

_____

_____

_____

Write Psalm 119:75–76 in your own words. Reflecting
on these verses and on Elizabeth's and Robyn's testimonies, write your own testimony of how God's Word is
your anchor.

_____

_____

Anchored by Peace

FEAR CAN BE a very destructive power in our lives. We live in a culture experiencing fear and anxiety at epidemic levels, and unfortunately, even God's people are not immune. Even the Bible gives us many examples of people who feared; even those who walked closest with Jesus, the disciples, expressed fear on several occasions.

In his devotional "The Rope of Life," Michael Youssef writes: "An ancient monastery sits on top of a cliff in the beautiful countryside of Portugal. Visitors to this lofty retreat are rewarded with a magnificent view. However, the only way to reach the monastery is by being hoisted up a cliff in a wicker basket by an aged monk.

One day, as a visitor prepared to leave, he turned to his guide and asked nervously, "How often do you replace this rope?" The gray-haired monk chimed, "Each time the old rope breaks."

Many times, this is exactly how we live. We push and shove our way through each day, worrying when the rope of life will break. Fear, doubt, and worry can paralyze us.

We may mistakenly think only nonbelievers live this way. However, many Christians are living the same.

Here is the wondrous truth of God: He holds the rope of our lives within His infinite, loving grasp. Nothing is strong enough to remove His shelter of protection from our lives. He knows our every move, and He is constantly aware of our deepest needs."

The question is, What do we do with fear and anxiety when it sneaks its way into our lives?

Worry comes from a German word for "choke or strangle." Worry chokes off our potential for living victorious lives and being who God intends us to be.

There is no greater anchor against those fears and anxieties—those storms that we face in this life—than the peace that comes from knowing and trusting in God. Maybe that is not good news for some of you reading this because you find the act of trusting pretty difficult. And yes, you're right; it is. Trusting God means that we have to give up that sense of control we feel we have over our lives. It means that we have to make the choice to put away the worry and the fear that we face. Because what else is worry and fear than two wicked little worms that give us the false sense of security that we can take care of any storm that comes our way? To put it a little bluntly, trusting God in the storms means—bottom line—to just hush up! Raise your hand if you struggle with that at all!

The peace that we are offered through our relationship with Christ anchors us in more than one way. First, we will see that there are times when during the middle of a storm we need to drop our anchor and just stand firm until the worst passes. Other times, we need to pull our anchor and head out to a safe haven. Third, there are times when God chooses to take the storm miraculously away. However, what we can never forget is this: Christ has complete authority over our lives, and it is His authority that determines whether we remain for a season in the storm or whether we are spared. In either case, He Himself is our peace; so no matter what, He can be trusted to take the best care of our souls. When we choose to battle Him, to try to find our own way out, to choose to be our own anchor, we just may find ourselves floundering around, causing destruction, and feeling washed away without a lifeboat.

In late June of 1994, I was spending some time with my cousin and her family at their condominium on the Gulf Coast between Alabama and Florida. The Sunday morning that I was scheduled to leave, we decided to take another boat ride out into the Gulf before I hit the road and headed home, which at the time was Shreveport. We loaded up in the boat and headed toward the beautiful, peaceful Gulf waters. The waters, however, were anything but peaceful on that particular morning. The water was beyond "a little choppy," causing the boat to lean every which way. When

we went through the pass, which would take
river into the actual Gulf, I got so nervous th.
moved from where I was sitting on the side of the
one of the lower seats. After we made it through .
the Gulf waters were not much better. I remember ⹂
ing my eyes on the shore the whole time in case we ⹂.
to swim for it. Finally, we realized that this boat ride was
turning into more of an ordeal than we anticipated, so we
turned around and headed back to the marina. When we
got back into the condominium, someone turned on the
television, and we discovered that there had been a tropical storm warning for our area. This tropical storm was the
infamous Alberto, which caused about $1 billion in damage
and thirty deaths across the Southeast.

I did not like this experience. It was really the only time
I've ever been frightened by the water. While I was on that
boat, I felt the danger of being at the mercy of the wind
and the waves. I saw what a powerful thing a storm is when
you're right in the middle of it. I wanted out! I wanted
the wind to die down and the waves to stop tossing us
around. I figured that wasn't likely to happen, so in the
meantime, I just had to trust the person piloting the boat
knew what he was doing because I knew I certainly was
not equipped to take the wheel and get us to safety. Though
my heart and my stomach and my thoughts were all being
bounced this way and that, I still had a sense of trust that

we were going to get safely back home. That's the kind of trust that the Lord wants us to have, I think. Not that we ignore the storm—no, we are fully aware of the power of life's storms in our lives—but we recognize His power over those storms.

In the Gospels, we read where the disciples faced a pretty scary storm when taking a boat from one side of the Sea of Galilee to the other. Mark's account tells us that there was a "fierce gale of wind, and the waves were breaking over the boat so much that the boat was already filling up" (Mark 4:37). The disciples were pretty frightened, and it's no wonder; these guys were used to being out on the water, and in this particular area, it isn't uncommon to experience these sudden winds and rainstorms. However, this particular storm had apparently taken on the properties of a hurricane. Some commentators even mention that the term "fierce gale" refers to a whirlwind or tornado. At any rate, they were not just frightened; they feared for their lives. But Jesus was so at peace that He was fast asleep on the cushions. That is, until the disciples woke Him up. (By the way, I think it's a little humorous that in all the accounts of this incident, the text reads "they" woke Him up. As if no one wanted to come clean on being the one to go wake Jesus up!)

In these passages (found in Matthew 8, Mark 4, and Luke 8), Jesus spoke to the winds and the sea, commanding

them to "Hush! Be still!" I kind of wonder if He was direct-
ing that same command to His disciples. After all, they
were just as stirred up as the sea by that point, and for them
to respond with such fear indicated their faith in Him still
had a long way to go. In a way, that makes me feel a little
bit better about those times when my faith shows itself to
be a little less mature than what I believe it to be. If they
could still have such fear after having Jesus in their physical
presence, then maybe I shouldn't beat myself up so badly
when I respond with fear and anxiety when life's storms
hit me unexpectedly. Matthew's Gospel tells us that Jesus
and His disciples had had a very busy day, and in Matthew
8:1–17, we read about several miracles of healing that Jesus
performed. So why didn't the disciples have more faith in
that boat?

One of the theories that I have is that all those other
situations involved someone else. That storm on the Sea
of Galilee involved them! Sometimes it is easier for us to
believe for others than to believe for ourselves. Sometimes
we don't have any trouble praying for others who are experiencing a storm and needing peace, but we just can't seem
to pray in faith for ourselves. This may have been the mind-
set that the disciples had—that Jesus came to save "all those
other people." But they were the Disciples. They were good,
thanks. Until that wind came up, and things got a little
gnarly in the boat. Then they themselves became mem-

bers of the universal "Whosoever Club," and some generic "they" finally got busy and woke Jesus up, realizing that He just might be able to do something about this situation.

Jesus in His compassion and mercy pointed out to them that their fear was getting in the way of their faith. All they needed was to trust Him, but He knew their struggle with that. All these strong-willed, self-made men that He had chosen for the strengths that He saw in them, He also saw the weaknesses that came with the territory and He loved His disciples nonetheless. Instead of tossing them out of the boat in the middle of the tempest in a gesture of "tough love," He very swiftly calmed their fears by calming the storm, reminding them that He is in complete control.

Later, as He preparing them for His crucifixion and resurrection (as He essentially said good-bye to them), He encouraged them by saying, "Peace I leave with you; My peace I give to you; not as the world gives do I give to you. Do not let your heart be troubled, nor let it be fearful" (John 14:27). Though there are many definitions of the word *peace*, here Jesus was referring to a sense of calm and rest, and He wanted the disciples to understand that there is a difference in the kind of peace that comes from blue skies and sunshiny days that we always hope to experience in this world and the kind of peace that He gives— the peace that transcends any storm or trial that we might face. Jesus knew there would be storms we would have to endure for long periods of time. I think of a friend who has a chronic illness that causes her pain and discomfort and great expense every day. She so wants to be free from this storm, but the Lord allows her to continue to experience His peace despite how badly she feels. I think of another friend who lives through the storm of loneliness every day. Despite her fear of being left alone without any support—emotional, financial, or otherwise—she has a great sense of peace that everyone around her senses. The peace that Jesus gives us, as He says, is not the kind of temporary comfort that the world offers, that pacifies us and distracts us during our struggles. No, His peace allows us to transcend life's storms.

In his book, *The Problem of Pain*, C. S. Lewis writes that "the security [peace] we crave would teach us to rest our hearts in this world...[however]...our Father refreshes us on the journey with some pleasant inns, but will not encourage us to mistake them for home." We do tend to mistake worldly things for our anchors, don't we? Friendships, wealth, health, good jobs, etc. can sometimes seem like they are the things that ground us and provide security for us in this world. But none of these things are really solid enough to be our anchors. Friends will disappoint us and we will disappoint them, wealth is iffy at best, and we can lose our health and our employment in the blink of an eye. However, one of my favorite passages in the Old Testament puts our worldly anchors in perspective: "Though the fig tree should not blossom and there be no fruit on the vines, though the yield of the olive should fail and the fields produce no food, though the flock should be cut off from the fold and there be no cattle in the stalls, yet I will exult in the Lord, I will rejoice in the God of my salvation. The Lord is my strength (*my anchor*), and He has made my feet like hinds' feet, and makes me walk on my high places" (Hab. 3:17–19, italics added). In other words, no matter what happens with all the things I may tend to put my trust in, only my God is truly my strength and my anchor.

In every storm that we go through, Jesus shows Himself to be our anchor and our peace, but not just for the sake of building our character or making us a good example for others. No, the stronger the storms we face, the stronger we grip our Anchor and the stronger our Anchor holds us steady. That, my friends, is the kind of trust He wants us to have.

Over the course of our days, we face many different types of storms, but they all have some of the same characteristics. First, even though not all storms are unexpected, they are always unpredictable. When the apostle Paul was being transported to Rome by ship, everyone knew they were traveling at a very dangerous time of year for sea travel in that area. Chapter 27 of Acts records the difficult and dangerous travel conditions that the ship carrying Paul and the other prisoners battled along the way. Finally, the ship reached a place called Fair Havens; but by this time, the weather was getting near impossible for travel. Paul took a chance and warned his captors that to continue the voyage at that time would result in great loss and damage. However, the ship's captain had a plan to get them to Phoenix, where they would wait out the winter before they continued to Rome. Then it got even nastier.

In Acts 27:13, we read, "When a moderate south wind came up, supposing that they had attained their purpose, they weighed anchor and began sailing along Crete, close inshore. But before very long there rushed down from the land a violent wind called Euraquilo; and when the ship was caught in it and could not face the wind, we gave way to it and let ourselves be driven along. Running under the shelter of a small island…we were scarcely able to get the ship's boat under control." The Euraquilo was what we would consider these days as a superstorm. It consisted of two separate storms coming together—one from the north and one from the east. Because this happened over water, the fluctuating temperatures made the storm even stronger. It was a pretty bad deal.

Even though it was well known they were headed into a difficult time, no one could predict with any accuracy just how bad of a time the ship would have. Eventually, they got to the point where all they could do was try to prepare for the next stage of "worse" by pulling the ship's dinghy up on board in the event they needed an escape.

Sometimes we can see a bad time coming. I'm reminded of those who have watched their children making a series of poor life choices that finally erupted into a major life crisis. I'm reminded of the women who make poor relationship choices, always aware of the risk of losing everything. Every day they anticipate the worst, never knowing when the storm will hit, only knowing that it will. Then one day, the worst happens, and they (and often their children) are left to sift through what's left of the destruction. Often, we are able to see financial crises coming at us as layoffs begin at work or investments are lost. What all of these have in common is that even though we may see them coming, we can't always predict the toll that they will take when they hit.

A mother knows that her son is involved with kids who claim to be in a gang. She would never imagine that her son would be involved in a drug-related shooting until the sheriff shows up at her house to take her to the hospital so that, hopefully, she can tell her mortally wounded son good-bye. A wife knows that her husband has been distant lately, finding reasons not to come home until late at night. She would never imagine that he is being unfaithful to her until she wakes up one morning and finds the divorce papers waiting for her. A mother knows that her son is mentally ill, and she is working through the process to get him the help that he needs before he hurts himself or others. But she would never imagine that he would take guns from her collection and kill her and six other adults as well as twenty young children. Thousands of Christians in the Middle East have watched powerlessly as Islamic militants have made their way closer and closer to their homes. They would never have imagined the destruction and poverty and loss they would suffer for the sake of Jesus. But now, they are waking every morning wondering if today is the day they will be martyred for their faith.

Like Paul and his shipmates, in storms like these sometimes all we can do is just give way to it, drop our anchor, and let ourselves be driven along with the storm (Acts 27:17). If we can see it coming, sometimes we can prepare as best we can. But the thing about storms is that we never know how to prepare. Here in Georgia, whenever there is any sort of possibility for the power to go off due to bad weather, people flock to the store for bread, milk, and water. People along the coast board up windows and bring in their patio furniture. None of these things stop the storms from hitting, but they give us a sense that we are prepared for them. Can we really prepare for the storms of loss and grief? No, but we can know that we have an Anchor to sustain us. We don't have to allow ourselves to be driven along by the winds and the rain. We can hold on to our Savior and know that He won't let us get blown too far off course.

All storms are unpredictable. Storms also disrupt our daily routines; they upset our "normal." Storms take away those things that bring us comfort or security. They take away our sense of control and our ability to rest. They are game changers, and they can definitely be life changers as well. They cause us to see our world, our relationships, ourselves, and our Savior through a different set of eyes. They give us a new perspective.

In Psalm 119, the psalmist testifies that suffering was what brought about a new desire for God's Word. He writes, "You have dealt well with Your servant, O Lord, according to Your word. Teach me good discernment and knowledge, for I believe in Your commandments. Before I was afflicted I went astray, but now I keep Your Word. You are good and do good; teach me Your statutes…It is good for me that I was afflicted, that I may learn Your statutes… I know, O Lord, that Your judgments are righteous, and that in faithfulness You have afflicted me. O may Your lovingkindness comfort me, according to Your word to Your servant. May Your compassion come to me that I may live, for Your law is my delight…Those who love Your law have great peace, and nothing causes them to stumble" (Ps. 119: 65–68, 71, 75–76, 165).

What the psalmist learned through the storm that he writes about in this passage is that there is no greater pursuit in all of life, no greater treasure, than the pursuit of following closely after God. Brennan Manning writes, "God wants us to be people who live close to Him, people for whom God is enough. That is the root of peace. We have that peace when the gracious God is all we seek. When we start seeking something besides Him, we lose that peace." Storms help us to gain this new perspective on life.

Storms also give us the chance to rebuild, and this is a really great thing. Though some may have to start from nothing, there is still hope for a better future when what is old has passed away and what is new can now replace it.

In Acts 27:18, the author, Luke, continues to describe this awful storm they were in the middle of. He writes, "The next day as we were being violently storm-tossed, they began to jettison the cargo; and on the third day they threw the ship's tackle overboard with their own hands. Since neither sun nor stars appeared for many days, and no small storm was assailing us, from then on all hope of our being saved was gradually abandoned." The men had become desperate. They were trying everything that they could think of to improve their chances of survival.

Sometimes it takes a major storm like this to show us the dead weight that we have in our lives that needs to be thrown overboard. Possessions or even relationships that we thought we couldn't live without may begin to seem pointless and worthless or may be seen as destructive factors in our lives. Maybe you have to downsize your home, selling or giving away items that you have been holding on to for years. Maybe you have to end destructive relationships or minimize the amount of time you spend with people who don't encourage you to do the right thing. Maybe a storm helps you to discover negative emotional baggage you are carrying around with you—perhaps an attitude that you suddenly realize is condescending or unnecessarily confrontational. Maybe you have unknowingly adopted some of the world's philosophies that are in conflict with the biblical principles that you want to guide your life. It's not a bad thing to off-load things that weigh us down. In fact, Hebrews 12:1 calls these things "encumbrances" and "sin which so easily entangles us."

How do we know what to throw overboard? We rely on the Lord to show us. I know that we have all probably experienced the fact that the darker the storm, the harder we pray. And as we pray, as we cling to our saving Anchor, He will show us those possessions, relationships, attitudes, and habits that are not pleasing to Him. Sometimes He uses a storm to show us something He couldn't show us in any other circumstance. It is our job to listen to His voice and to obey.

I have heard His voice in a variety of ways. I have heard Him through His Word and through prayer. Sometimes it is through a sermon or a Sunday School or Bible study lesson. Sometimes He will speak to me through another person, whether it's a friend or even a stranger who may say something unknowingly that speaks directly to my heart. I remember once, when I was going through a difficult time in my career and really struggling with which direction I needed to follow, I received an e-mail from someone that had known me in one of my earlier capacities in the ministry. She e-mailed me out of the blue, and in the course of the e-mail, she happened to ask me if I still did any writing. At the time, I had to admit to her that I did not. This was actually something the Lord had been impressing upon me to do during that particular season in my life, but I had just kept putting it off. Receiving that message from this person from my past affirmed the direction that I felt the Lord was leading me to and gave me a little extra encouragement to get busy. Hearing from the Lord through this old friend reaffirmed to me that He had not abandoned me, that He was still leading me, and that He would continue to put me where He wanted me. That e-mail was His reminder to follow the convictions that He had been trying to impress upon me; He just knew, I suppose, that I needed to hear it from multiple directions. There are many ways we can hear His voice in the middle of a storm, and in His grace and mercy, He will make sure that we don't miss His call.

Job 37 says, "Listen closely to the thunder of His voice, and the rumbling that goes out from His mouth. Under the whole heaven He lets it loose, and His lightning to the ends of the earth. After it, a voice roars; He thunders with His majestic voice, and He does not restrain the lightnings when His voice is heard. God thunders with His voice wondrously, doing great things which we cannot comprehend...Whether for correction, or for His world, or for loving kindness, He causes it to happen" (Job 37:2–5, 13). Then in Job 38:1, we read that the Lord answered Job's questions by speaking to him through a whirlwind.

There are those who look at the destruction that major storms like Alberto, Katrina, or Hurricane Sandy leave behind and ask why God would use such a means to speak to His people. As awful as the aftermath of such storms is, the gracious and loving nature of God is not changed. He gets our attention with storms like this. He reminds us of His power, yes; but He also reminds us of His gentleness toward us, of His provision. He doesn't expect us to understand it, and we would save ourselves a lot of heartache if we would stop trying to understand and instead work on trusting Him more. I love the words He speaks to Job when He says, "Now gird up your loins like a man, and I will ask you, and you shall instruct Me!" In other words, "If you think you're qualified, go ahead and try to tell me what I should do!" John MacArthur explains this part of the one-sided conversation this way: "God silenced Job's presumption in constantly wanting to ask the questions of God by becoming Job's questioner. It must be noted that God never told Job about the reason for his pain...He never gave Job any explanation at all about the circumstances of his trouble. He did one thing in all He said. He asked Job if he was as eternal, great, powerful, wise, and perfect as God. If not, Job would have been better off to be quiet and trust him."

It is natural to want to understand why we go through some of the storms that we face. And it is not unheard of to go to God with those questions. But when having the answers upsets our sense of peace, we are really just creating a stronghold of distrust in our hearts, and this just totally contradicts what God wants to do in us. We cannot secure our own peace by understanding. God gives us our peace! (John 14:27) We may excuse our insistent questioning by saying that we want to understand so that we can be sure to do what God wants us to do. But that "need to know" mentality really is just a ploy of ours to grab the wheel and start trying to steer the ship again instead of just sitting under the shadow of the Almighty and trusting Him to get us through.

The one thing that Christians should never throw overboard in the middle of life's storms, however, is our hope. Acts 27:20 tells us that they gradually abandoned all hope of ever being saved. No matter how severe the storm is that we are facing, the Anchor that we have ensures we will come through it. And because we have this hope of ultimate security, we can have an unmistakable and unexplainable peace no matter how rough the storm is. Also, the hope we have serves as encouragement to others as well. In verses 21–25, Paul told the men to stay courageous, God had given him a vision that none of them would lose their lives. Because of Paul's faith in God and because he had not lost hope of reaching his destination, he was able to communicate this message to the men with confidence. Though he was a prisoner being delivered to his destination in order to stand trial, Paul became a leader on that ship for the duration of the journey because of the bravery and the underlying peace that he exhibited while everyone else was in a panic. No matter how strong the storms of our lives are, God's peace is so much stronger. It's truly a peace that defies understanding.

When I think of this unexplainable peace, I can't help but think of my sweet friend Kim. Here is her story of how God gave her a supernatural peace to get through an unspeakable storm in her life:

> On April 19, 2004, the unthinkable happened. My seventeen-year-old son died in an automobile accident. The moments after the phone call will forever define me and my walk with God. I know I am a Christian. I know I am a believer, but when you have to put your faith

to the test and live what you believe, that is when you have to trust God completely.

On the day of the funeral when everyone was around and all eyes were on me to see how I was going to react, all I wanted to do was go back home and crawl back into my bed and never leave again. I sat quietly in my seat and listened to all the wonderful things being said about my son and the songs being sung and thought, How can this be? How can the world still be moving forward? Then the time came, and the pastor had an altar call. I looked at my husband, and I asked, "Do you think it would be okay if I went?" He responded, "Of course you can." I made my way to the altar, to the amazement of everyone in the room. I knelt there before God, and the only words I could utter were "Give me peace, Lord. Give me peace." In those next few moments, the room grew quiet. There was no sound. It was just me and God, and he answered my prayer. He gave me just that peace. I was able to take a deep breath. I was able to see that life would move forward with his love and guidance. God was with me.

After that peaceful encounter, I was able to continue to worship God each day and praise him for the many blessings He continued to give me and my family even through the tragedy. I am still struggling with the loss, but God has opened many doors through the years to allow me to share with others who have lost their children how He has helped me find peace so that they may seek Him for their peace in their trial as well.

After all these years, Kim has come to understand that the only anchor she can hold on to through all the moments of grief she has experienced from losing her son is the anchor of peace. It is God's peace that helps her get through her days, knowing His presence is always with her, that He is holding on to her even when she doesn't feel that she can hold on any longer. Like Kim, in those moments, His peace overtakes us and keeps us from falling apart. But most importantly, His peace keeps us close to Him, which is exactly where we need to be when life's storms overwhelm us.

Just one final word about this anchor of peace: we live in a world where peace seems to be in short supply. Too often, I find that people equate peace with satisfaction, and I need to stress this is certainly not the case. Like the earlier quote from C. S. Lewis, we are not to find our security and satisfaction in the things or the people of this world; when we try to do so, we will end up being very disappointed and very dissatisfied. My admonition to you is this: don't just be at peace with God but be at peace with others as well—not because it will make your life better but because it is what God expects of His people (Rom. 12:18). Being at peace with others means we choose to show people mercy and grace even when they've wronged us. It means being forgiving toward others rather than holding an offense against them. Mostly, I think being at peace with others shows that we are able to look beyond their sins and weaknesses and see them as God sees them—a person deserving of kindness and unconditional love and acceptance, even on their worst days. God has made a way for all of us to be at peace with Him, even the worst of us at our worst. We must do the same for others.

For those who are going through a storm right now, whether an illness, a broken relationship, a financial crisis, or whatever it might be, God's Word has a message for you. The apostle Paul writes, "For I consider that the sufferings of this present time are not worthy to be compared with the glory that is to be revealed to us" (Rom. 8:18). And "we exult in our tribulations, knowing that tribulation brings about perseverance; and perseverance, proven character; and proven character, hope; and hope does not disappoint, because the love of God has been poured out within our hearts through the Holy Spirit who was given to us" (Rom. 5:3–4). Notice that last part: God has poured His love out in our hearts—not trickled it out, not just a little sprinkle, but a flat-out downpour! No matter what you're going through, just hold on to the anchor of peace that comes through Jesus Christ.

Learn It and Live It: Anchored by Peace

What would you say is your greatest fear? How does fear make you feel?

_____

_____

_____

_____

_____

Are there times when you feel more anxious than others? Explain?

_____

_____

_____

_____

_____

What makes you feel the most secure?

_____

_____

_____

_____

_____

What are the differences between security and peace? How
are they similar?

_____

_____

_____

_____

_____

Read the account of Jesus calming the storm from Matthew 8:23–27, Mark 4:35–41, and Luke 8:22–25. Describe what happened in your own words and then answer the questions below.

_____

_____

_____

_____

_____

The Gospels tell us that the disciples' response was fear and amazement. What do you think they were seeing about Jesus in this situation that they hadn't seen before?

_____

_____

_____

_____

_____

Read Matthew 8:1–17. What else had the disciples witnessed Jesus do that day? Do you think they should have been stronger by this point? What was different about this incident in the boat? Are there times when it is easier for you to have faith for others than to believe what Jesus can accomplish in your own life?

_____

_____

_____

_____

_____

Read John 14:27. The word for "peace" in the previous verses literally means "hush," but the word in this verse means "a sense of calm." Think about the difference between those two words and situations in your life when you might need each of them or both applied.

_____

_____

_____

_____

_____

Describe a time when you asked Jesus to give you peace. Were you asking for the "hush" kind or the "calm" kind? What was the situation? How did He answer?

_____

_____

_____

_____

_____

Read Habakkuk 3:17–19. The passage lists things that were strongly relied on by the people to give them a sense of security, but the writer's point was that there will come a time when those things will fail. What did he say his response would be even when those sources of security were gone?

_____

_____

_____

_____

_____

What are some things in your life that you have used as
a substitute for the anchor of peace that Christ supplies?
What finally made you realize that this substitute was
not sufficient?

_____

_____

_____

_____

_____

Read Acts 27:1–12. The sailors knew they were traveling
at a dangerous time (think taking a cruise during peak
hurricane season), but they ignored the potential dangers
and went on with their plans. What are some danger signs
that the Lord gives you that a storm may be headed your
way? When He gives a warning, how do you think you
should respond?

_____

_____

_____

_____

_____

Read Acts 27:13–20. The passage describes the men on the ship preparing for the worst by throwing things overboard. Going through a turbulent time can show you things in your life that are pulling you down, whether sinful habits, relationships, or possessions. Name a time when the Lord took you through a storm that led you to throw some "deadweight" overboard.

_____

_____

_____

_____

_____

In verse 20, we read that the men on the ship gradually lost hope of ever being saved. When has life been that bad for you? How did God come through for you? Are you going through a time like that now? What anchor can you hold on to that will keep you from losing hope?

_____

_____

_____

_____

_____

Read Psalm 119:65–68. What hope does this passage give for going through difficulties in life?

_____

_____

_____

_____

_____

Read Acts 27:21–25. How did God remind Paul of His presence with them in the storm? How did this give hope to the others?

———————————————————

———————————————————

———————————————————

———————————————————

———————————————————

Is it okay to question God when we experience storms? What should be our ultimate attitude when it comes to this? Read Job 37:2–5, 13.

———————————————————

———————————————————

———————————————————

———————————————————

———————————————————

Anchored by Freedom

IT'S QUITE UNFORTUNATE that the way you usually figure out you have a phobia of something is when you experience it. And freak out. I never knew that I was claustrophobic until I took a bad fall and ended up in the MRI tube. Luckily I was in an open MRI, so I was able to turn my head enough to look out; but until I discovered that little trick, I was a little panicky to say the least. It was like being buried alive! My body's fight-or-flight response was going crazy, but in order to get out of there, I had to stay still for nearly an hour. Periodically, the technician would speak to me and encourage me that yes, time was passing and that the ordeal would be over "soon"; but still, I felt trapped, and I wanted out. That little open area above my head where I could look out and see freedom was the only thing that kept me from crawling out of there!

There is just something about being confined, being restrained, or being in a position where you don't have control over whether you can move or not. This is, for me, what can trigger a panic attack. It is the sense that something can happen to you and you won't have the opportunity to remove yourself from the situation. You sense your control has been taken away. Your mind triggers your body to produce chemicals in abundance that prepare you with the energy you need to either fight off the threat or escape it. Your heart starts pounding, your skin grows clammy, and your breathing becomes labored—as if you are running a marathon—all because you sense a loss of control.

Realistically, though, this sense that we are in control of our lives is merely an illusion. We think that as adults, we have the freedom to make our own choices about everything. To a certain extent, that is true. We choose what clothes we want to wear, what books we want to read, what type of car we want to drive, and what foods we want to eat. But as you are searching the department store for the right outfit or shopping for food at the supermarket, have you ever wondered who decided the selection you have to choose from? Sure, you can go to another store; but still, the choices you make are limited to the items available to you. So then, the idea that you are expressing your personal style by the clothes and jewelry you choose to wear is somewhat of a delusion because whatever style you choose has actually already been chosen for you. Someone, somewhere is aware of the variety of tastes that people have; they know the types of things that will appeal to you or not, and they make sure the variety of items they offer will appeal to the greatest number of people in any given area. It's called merchandising, and it's done brilliantly because most of us are not even consciously aware of it. Every time you try on an outfit and exclaim, "I love it!" a merchandiser has hit a homerun. Not only do the merchandisers tailor their selection to our tastes, the marketing industry actually has a huge influence in shaping our tastes. Every time we make a choice for a certain product, we are affirming the influence marketing has over us. Are you kind of getting the picture of how many of our choices are under the control of someone we will likely never even know exists?

There is a spiritual parallel to this concept that we are rarely conscious of, and that is the fact that every time we make a personal choice, we are revealing who is in control of us spiritually. The Bible refers to this control as spiritual slavery. In Romans 6:16–18, the apostle Paul wrote, "Do you not know that when you present yourselves to someone as slaves for obedience, you are slaves of the one whom you obey, either of sin resulting in death, or of obedience resulting in righteousness? But thanks be to God that though you were slaves of sin, you became obedient from the heart to that form of teaching to which you were committed, and having been freed from sin, you became slaves of righteousness."

In John 8:31–36, Jesus was having a conversation with some of the Jews who had believed in Him. He told them,

"If you continue in My word, then you are truly disciples of Mine; and you will know the truth, and the truth will make you free." The Jewish people were confused by this and asked Jesus, "How can you say that we will become free if we have never yet been enslaved to anyone?" Jesus responded to them, "Everyone who commits sin is the slave of sin. The slave does not remain in the house forever; the son does remain forever. So if the Son makes you free, you will be free indeed." Paul emphasized this when he wrote, "For the law of the Spirit of life in Christ Jesus has set you free from the law of sin and of death" (Rom. 8:2).

Usually when Christians think of being a slave to sin, we think of it in terms of being in bondage to particular sins. Even "good" church people struggle with addictions to drugs, alcohol, pornography or other sexual sins, with food addictions or eating disorders, with anger issues, unforgiveness, bitterness, or other destructive behaviors. But in these passages, it is clear that the bondage that is described is bondage to the power of the sinful condition itself, and since both of these passages are being addressed to the religious people, it is also clear that even those who believe that they are doing everything right can sometimes be under the bondage of sin. We ask, "How can that be?" How is it that we can be trying so hard to be right with God and still not be right with God?

In doing counseling at church, the first question I usually ask, even of people that I already know, is about their relationship with Jesus Christ. Surprisingly, the response to that question usually begins with the statement "I was baptized..." This can sometimes be a pretty revealing response because if baptism is the person's first thought when they think of beginning a relationship with Christ, this might indicate they have gotten some spiritually foundational things out of order. Here's the thing: the freedom we have through faith in Christ has nothing to do with what we have done and everything to do with what He has done. But so often, we forget that very important truth, and we begin to work harder and harder to measure up. In his book *One Way Love: Inexhaustible Grace for an Exhausted World*, Tullian Tchividjian writes, "Jesus came to liberate us from the weight of having to make it on our own, from the demand to measure up. He came to emancipate us from the burden to get it all right, from the obligation to fix ourselves, find ourselves, and free ourselves. Jesus came to release us from the slavish need to be right, rewarded, regarded, and respected. Because Jesus came to set the captives free, life does not have to be a tireless effort to establish ourselves, justify ourselves, and validate ourselves." The Lord used a Bible study to show my friend Jackie that even though she had been working really hard to "do church," she had actually missed a critical step. Here's her story:

I was saved at age eleven, or so I thought. As a child, I went to church occasionally. In my teen years, I went to church with a friend just to play softball. As an adult, I went to church in spurts. After my children were born, I realized they needed to be in church, so my daughters and I started attending on a regular basis.

I taught Sunday School. I helped with children's choir on Sunday nights and led children in Mission Kids on Wednesday nights. In 2007, my husband was saved, and we started attending church as a family. I was at the church every time the doors were open. I was attending Bible studies, Sunday School, and church as well as helping in AWANA, helping in the kitchen, and serving on the Women's Ministry Team. I was doing anything to serve.

In a very personal Bible study, "Experiencing God," I realized something. I did not know Jesus as my Lord and Savior, though all this time I thought I had it all together serving and teaching. One Sunday morning during the altar call, I looked at my husband and said, "I don't know if I truly know who God is." He looked at me confused and said, "What?" I said, "I don't know who God is."

He took my hand and we went to the preacher and I prayed that God would come into my heart and be the Lord and Savior of my life. Since that time, the words

*in the Bible just flow off the page. I may not understand
everything I read all the time, but now it all makes
more sense—now more than ever before.*

*After I was truly saved and took communion for the
first time, I realized that this bread was a symbol of
His body and that the juice was a symbol of His blood
that He gave for me and you. I just sat there with chills
realizing that He loves me so much and that He died for
me. That He has been the anchor in my life even before
I realized it. God gives us freedom over our sin when
we follow Him.*

*With all this said, it is never too late to give your
heart to Jesus.*

God revealed to Jackie that what she had been doing
all along was basically trying to do the right thing with
the wrong motivation. She was trying to create her own
righteousness by doing the "right" things according to the
standard of the institution of the church without actually
being a part of the body of the Church. But the kind of
righteousness that God requires—perfect righteousness—
is something that we can never obtain for ourselves.

What Jesus did for us on the cross accomplished an
amazing thing, and it is so important that we understand
all this means for us. Having said that, let me give this
disclaimer: we will never fully understand it. C. S. Lewis,

in *Mere Christianity*, puts this so well: "Christ's death has somehow put us right with God and given us a fresh start...We believe that the death of Christ is just the point in history at which something absolutely unimaginable from outside shows through into our own world. And if we cannot picture even the atoms of which our own world is built, of course we are not going to be able to picture this."

I am reminded of a passage in the Old Testament where we are provided a clear picture of Christ freeing His people from their chains. In Daniel 3, King Nebuchadnezzar commanded everyone in his kingdom to bow down to a golden image that he had created. However, three of the Israelites serving in his court refused to comply with this command. Enraged by the refusal of Shadrach, Meshach, and Abednego to worship the golden image, the king had the three men tied up and thrown into the blazing furnace. Daniel 3:23 states that "these three men...fell into the midst of the furnace of blazing fire still tied up." However, as the king gazed into the furnace, he saw something that was unexplainable by any human means. Nebuchadnezzar told his officials, "'Was it not three men we cast bound into the midst of the fire?' They replied to the king, 'Certainly, O king.' He said, 'Look! I see four men loosed and walking about in the midst of the fire without harm, and the appearance of the fourth is like a son of the gods!'" Likely, the fourth person in the fire, the one who broke the bonds the men were tied up in, was Christ Himself. Christ meets us in the midst of the fire and frees us from the chains of sin and death. Only He could do this. Just as these three young men were powerless to save themselves from the fire, we are powerless to save ourselves from the penalty of sin, and thank God that He does so not based on any merit in ourselves, but based solely on His grace, His mercy, and His faithfulness.

In fact, in the fifth chapter of Romans, Paul writes that we were once enemies with God. This has been a concept that is hard for this church girl to fathom, but it's the truth nonetheless. By being born into this sinful world, I was born an enemy of God, helpless to make right my relationship with Him. But the wonderful truth of the Gospel is because of the death of Christ, the penalty for my sin (death) has been completely paid and I have been made right. I have gone from being God's enemy to being His daughter. Romans 5:1 says "having been justified by faith, we have peace with God through our Lord Jesus Christ." And the thing that makes it even more remarkable is what Paul writes in Romans 5:6–8: "For while we were still helpless, at the right time Christ died for the ungodly. For one will hardly die for a righteous man; though perhaps for the good man someone would dare even to die. *But God demonstrates His own love for us, in that while we were yet sinners [His enemies!] Christ died for us*" (emphasis added).

Justification is a wonderful thing. It means God has declared us to be free from the penalty of sin. As a result, we are now at peace with Him, and we are restored to a right relationship with Him. John MacArthur writes, "God has declared Himself to be at war with every human being because of man's sinful rebellion against Him and His laws. But the first great result of justification is that the sinner's war with God is ended forever." What wonderful news this is for us! We no longer have to try to create our own righteousness or to make ourselves right with God. When we try, we always end up feeling a failure because it's impossible for us to do. All we have to do is accept this gift of God's grace through faith. And even the very faith that we need to believe doesn't have to be self-generated because He gives us even that! (Eph. 2:8–9)

Because Jesus Christ anchors us in His freedom, we no longer have to live in the bondage of sin, the bondage of self-effort, and the bondage of "good enough." He has made us right.

How is it that even we Christians get tangled up in the chains of this world? How is it we can let our lives get so far offtrack that they hardly resemble anything the Lord intends for us?

Here's a question for you: When was the last time you heard the word "fornication?" There may be some of you reading this who have never heard this word and some for whom it's been so long you had to stop and Google it. It's a word that is rarely used in the church anymore because so few people recognize there is anything wrong with sex outside of marriage, and using such a word seems arcane and a little judgmental. Just because we've stopped calling it sin doesn't make it less of a sin, and it doesn't remove its consequences. Sexual sin destroys relationships and breaks up marriages, and it can have some devastating physical and emotional consequences, such as unwanted pregnancies, sexually transmitted diseases, and sexual addictions. And herein lies my point: Christians get tangled up in the chains of this world because we have stopped talking about sin. We think we have our "Jesus life" all tidied up, in its box, and ready to put on when we have a need to be spiritual. But for the most part, we just live our lives without ever considering the concept of sin. We have our church life and our church friends, but we have our day-to-day life as well. But acknowledging sin as sin puts us in the posture to confess our sin to God, to repent of our sin, and to experience His forgiveness and cleansing. Calling sin *sin* isn't meant to be a shaming experience, though there will likely be some shame involved. Calling sin *sin* is a great source of hope for us, and it is the only way we can experience freedom from it. After all, how can we be freed from chains we don't even know are restraining us?

Jerry Bridges, in 2007, wrote a book titled *Respectable Sins*. In it, he discusses how the concept of sin is disappearing from our culture and even from our churches. Things which were once considered sin to the Christian community but also wrong from a moral standpoint within the culture are now considered acceptable. Bridges says that he believes the sin of ungodliness to be the root cause of all our other sins, and it is a sin that all of us are guilty of to some degree. He writes, "Does that statement surprise you, or maybe even offend you? We don't think of ourselves as ungodly. After all, we *are* Christians; we are not atheists or wicked people. We attend church, avoid scandalous sins, and lead respectable lives. In our minds, the ungodly folks are the ones who live truly wicked lives. How, then, can I say that we believers are all, to some extent, ungodly?" Bridges's definition of ungodliness is living your life with very little thought of God. We may read our Bible or spend a few minutes in prayer, but the rest of our day-to-day lives are pretty much free of any thought of God at all. This thought, when I first read it, brought such conviction to me. Then as I read through the following chapters of the book, I realized how little I allowed God to impact my life on a moment-by-moment basis. And here I was, not only a faithful Christian but serving in full-time Christian service and yet still living many of my days with nothing more than lip service to Christ. Here are some of the sins that Bridges lists as "respectable sins," those sins that we not only accept in ourselves but also tend to overlook in others as well: anxiety and frustration, discontentment, unthankfulness, pride, selfishness, lack of self control, impatience and irritability, anger, judgmentalism, envy and jealousy, sins of the tongue, and worldliness.

The thing about these sins is we tend to get caught up in them gradually, and then before we know it, we have been pulled in so deep that it's hard to see our way out. If we don't recognize them, repent of them, and replace them with godly virtues, then slowly but surely these sinful attitudes and behaviors will increase in our lives until we look down and see that we are completely chained by them. Let's take the sin of worldliness as an example. One expression of this sin is overspending. Despite all the financial instruction in the Bible, the average credit card debt in America is $16,000. Credit card debt can be so life-dominating that it can actually cause physical illness. But what causes it? Essentially, it is the practice of living beyond your means. Carrying a credit card balance that is so high creates physical stress and relational stress and is reflective, often, of a dissatisfied heart.

It is one of those sins that start out small. You make one purchase on credit, and you get that feeling of instant gratification. That item may sit in its box for months. But you have it. It's yours. It has filled some need you thought you had or some desire that you felt you wanted to fulfill in the moment. And then the next purchase is made, and the next. Soon, it becomes not only about being able to say of something, "Oh, yes, I own one of those!" But it becomes about seeking after contentment by accumulating things, things that can never bring contentment. In the meantime, the credit card balance grows until even the minimum payment is a stretch for your budget, and you are experiencing the full weight of the chain of worldliness.

The sin of impatience is another "respectable sin." In fact, I think this is likely to be the sin I most often hear excused. Impatience is born from a self-centered heart, from a heart that says, "My time is so important that I can't afford to waste it waiting on someone or something that isn't going to serve me immediately." I know someone who gets so impatient in traffic that she will take a detour that adds miles to her trip just to avoid red lights (because apparently, for her, stop signs are optional). I have known people in my life who have been proud of their impatience and laughed and shrugged it off as if it's merely a personality trait that they can't help. But you see, God expects His people to be patient just as He is patient with us. So when we refuse this and make light of it, then we are experiencing the chain of impatience.

Dishonesty is another chain that people are bound by. Every time we tell a lie or act in a dishonest way, this chain gets tighter and stronger. Dishonesty affects every relationship that we have because its roots go very deep into our hearts, and some say that the more we lie, the more we program our brains to avoid the truth—thus the person who lies habitually does so even when honesty would have a better outcome. Proverbs 6:16–19 lists the seven things that God hates, and on that list, two of them refer to dishonesty: a lying tongue (v. 17) and a false witness who utters lies (v. 19). Do you see the progression there? First, he hates the lying tongue—just the part of the body that communicates the deception. But in verse 19, he hates the false witness himself. This shows that, if we are not careful to avoid it, the sin of dishonesty can become so ingrained in us that it will define us.

Gluttony is another word that we don't often hear used anymore, but overeating and irresponsible eating habits are a very destructive sin that binds so many Christians today. Food has become an acceptable "drug" in the lives of many women. Food is used as a salve for hurt feelings, for stress relief, and even for companionship. Not only does the sin of overeating cause obvious health problems but it is also such a silent sin that binds our bodies that it is often hard to overcome. Our culture has become so well-informed about the importance of making wise diet choices, and yet 35 percent of Americans are obese. Overeating, like many life-dominating sins, seems so harmless; but when food begins to play a preeminent role in our lives, it's an idol of gluttony and keeps us from living a life honoring God.

What is the solution when we have identified sin in our lives? The Bible tells us that we are to confess our sin to God. To confess doesn't just mean to admit that we've sinned. Confession is agreeing with God about the ugliness of the sin we've committed. Confession is not the time to be defensive or to shift the blame to another person or even to God. It's an act that should be done with great humility and reverence. Repentance is another required part of the action plan. To repent means to immediately stop doing what you're doing and to completely turn and walk away from it. When we walk away from sin, we have to remember that we are walking toward righteousness. So for every sin we leave behind, we are to pick up a habit of godliness. For example, we replace overspending money with saving and with giving. We replace dishonesty with telling the truth, and so on. Confession and repentance together involve getting our mind, our heart, and our will on the same page. We change our mind about the acceptability of our sinful behavior, we allow our hearts to be cleansed, and we allow the Lord's will to replace our own will so we can walk in our newfound righteousness.

Sometimes, we don't even know we are bound by the chains of this life until we experience what it's like to be free of them. Here's my friend Jaime's story. See if any of it sounds familiar to you:

It was during a revival at a church in Milledgeville, Georgia, where I gave my life to Christ and accepted Him as my Savior—or so I thought. I was thirteen, and while the preacher, Rev. Terry Cliett, was giving the sermon, I became so overwhelmed with emotion that I just sat in that pew and cried. I went to him after service and explained that I had no idea where these emotions were coming from and was completely confused. He counseled me and led the prayer that gave me salvation. It would be twenty years before I truly understood what it meant to be a child of God and would know just how amazing salvation is.

My story is like many others. I lived my life according to what made me happy and as long as I wasn't hurting anyone, everything was okay. Right? Wrong! When life hits, it hits hard and can bring you to your lowest if you continue down the wrong path, regardless of how well intended you were. At thirty-one, I found myself feeling alone, abandoned, broken, and hopeless. A failed marriage and three kids—life looked so bleak. I was led back into church when my brother suggested I find a church to at least get out of the house and have something to do. I found so much more.

I began attending what is now my home church and found so much love and hope. But most of all, I real-

ized the importance of salvation. Through fellowship, I learned that I was not hopeless but hopeful; I was not abandoned because God never abandons His children; I was not broken but was being pieced back together by my Savior. He molded me into a work of art that He could proudly call His own.

Fully understanding and embracing my salvation has changed my life. It means more than reading my Bible, attending worship services, or even leading a children's Sunday School class. I am able to fully forgive those who have wronged me because I have been forgiven. I can love my enemy as well as my neighbor because I have been loved by Christ. My life has a purpose and meaning, something I never fully embraced until I fully embraced my Savior.

How do we break these chains that life and our choices wrap us in? We can't. And thankfully, we don't have to try. Christ does this for us, just as he did for those three Hebrew boys in that fiery furnace. The freedom that we have in Christ isn't just for our initial salvation and justification. He offers freedom from the sins that bind us in this life. It is part of the sanctifying work He does in His people to help us to live holy lives. Trying to break these chains can exhaust us. I have seen so many try to do it themselves. They exert as much willpower as they can create, and they do well—until something happens and they have a setback. It just doesn't work until we put our trust in the power of God. Tullian Tchividjian writes, "One way to summarize God's message to the worn out and weary is like this—God's demand: 'be righteous'; God's diagnosis—'no one is righteous'; God's deliverance—'Jesus is your righteousness.' Once this good news grips your heart, it changes everything. It frees you from having to be perfect. It frees you from having to hold it together." It frees you from your chains.

So once we are anchored in this freedom from the chains of sin, how do we live our lives? Paul tells us in Romans 6 that now that we are no longer slaves to sin, we become slaves to righteousness. What exactly does that mean?

One of my favorite passages of Scripture is in the book of Jude in verses 20–25: "But you, beloved, building your-selves up on your most holy faith, praying in the Holy Spirit, keep yourselves in the love of God, waiting anx-iously for the mercy of our Lord Jesus Christ to eternal life. And have mercy on some, who are doubting; save others, snatching them out of the fire; and on some have mercy with fear, hating even the garment polluted by the flesh. Now to Him who is able to keep you from stumbling, and to make you stand in the presence of His glory blameless with great joy, to the only God our Savior, through Jesus

Christ our Lord, be glory, majesty, dominion and authority, before all time and now and forever. Amen."

This passage gives an overview of how we are to live in freedom as Christians in this world. We are to build on the foundation Christ has laid for us by remaining faithful to Him and by maintaining a consistent prayer life so as to stay close to Him. We are to "keep ourselves in the love of God" or, in other words, to remain in the posture of obedience and faithfulness to Him, that place where we experience the pouring out of God's love, as opposed to being disobedient and experiencing His discipline. Then Jude discusses how we are to relate with others who may have a negative influence on us—sincere doubters who need our compassion, those who are struggling with unbelief who need our encouragement, and those who have turned away from the faith, that we are to treat with mercy while keeping an emotional distance in order to avoid being pulled away from Christ. Finally, we are to live a life of worship, praising and glorifying Christ for our salvation until we are able to stand in front of Him in Heaven.

To sum this passage up in terms I can understand, basically, just don't be careless with your soul or with the souls of others. Live your life with as much attention to obedience as possible in the power and love of God, letting your life overflow with His goodness and faithfulness to all those you encounter on your journey.

Christ didn't secure our freedom on the cross of Calvary so that we can do whatever we want without a thought for holiness. In fact, time after time, as we've seen here, living the life the world tells us is "fun" and "fulfilling" is anything but a life of freedom and is anything but "fulfilling." He secured our freedom so that we don't have to be in bondage to sin—a bondage that carries a death sentence for all eternity. His freedom anchors us to Himself; He keeps us protected, loved, and cherished. His freedom is life, and abundant life at that, for now and for eternity. Our Savior is the only one who can truly make us free indeed.

Learn It and Live It: Anchored by Freedom

Using your own words, give your personal definition of "freedom."

_____

_____

_____

_____

_____

Read Romans 6:16–18 then answer the questions below.
What is spiritual slavery?

_____

_____

_____

_____

_____

According to this passage we have two choices of spiritual
masters. What are they?

_____

_____

_____

_____

_____

In what way do we indicate who we have chosen as master?

_____

_____

_____

_____

_____

Read John 8:31–36. Summarize the conversation that Jesus was having with the Jewish people.

Who did Jesus say was a slave to sin?

_____

_____

_____

_____

_____

What is the difference between the son and the slave?

_____

_____

_____

_____

_____

Jesus speaks of the son and the Son (Himself). When He frees us from sin, our status changes from "slave" to "son." With that in mind, what do you think He means by the phrase "free, indeed"?

_____

_____

_____

_____

_____

Have you ever been truly freed from the bondage of your sinful condition? How did that happen in your life? Take a moment to reflect on this and write out your experience below. If you haven't ever placed your faith for salvation in Christ and experienced the freedom only He can give, now is the time for you to make that decision. Stop and turn to the next section of the book to find out how you can do that right now.

_____

_____

_____

_____

_____

Read Romans 5. Look up the definitions of any words you want to know more about and write them with their meanings below. As you read, note the main ideas of the chapter in the space below or in the margins of your Bible. Summarize the verses that stand out to you and tell what they mean to you.

_____

_____

_____

_____

_____

Take some time to reread the section in the chapter about common sins that we often excuse in our lives. As you read, ask the Lord to reveal to you any areas where you have allowed yourself to be bound by holding on to sin. What actions do you think you should take?

_____

_____

_____

_____

_____

Define "confession." What is the difference between confessing our sin and admitting that we have sinned?

_____

_____

_____

_____

_____

Define "repentance." When we walk away from sin, what are we to walk toward?

_____

_____

_____

_____

_____

Read Jude 20–25. Describe in your own words what the life of freedom in Christ looks like.

_____

_____

_____

_____

_____

List at least three ways that you can specifically apply the instruction in Jude 20–25 in your life.

_____

_____

_____

_____

_____

Final Thoughts

HOW CAN WE trust in the anchor of peace when our world is filled with war, racial bias, and hate crimes? How can we trust in the anchor of love when real love has been replaced with lust and infatuation and self-centered philosophies? How can we trust in the anchor of truth when so many churches and religious people are rewriting the Scriptures to appease the minds of people who just want affirmation for the way they want to live their lives? How can we trust in the anchor of freedom when there are Christians all over the world who are being persecuted, imprisoned, and martyred for their faith in Jesus?

Throughout history, God's people have experienced opposition and will continue to experience it. Amazingly, it is usually those areas where persecution is greatest where the Gospel spreads the fastest. Those areas are devoid of any hope, peace, or grace, except for the hope and peace and grace shown by the people of God. Remember the story of Paul and Silas in the Philippian prison (Acts 16:16–34).

They used their time in jail to have a worship service! God miraculously loosed their chains, and by the end of the night, their prison guard and his whole family had been saved and baptized! The chains that God's people wear for His sake can never take away the freedom that Christ gives.

We must remember that Satan will use his tools in this world to imitate what Christ offers. But none of his imitations will ever measure up to what Christ offers. Satan's anchors don't hold. They tarnish, they offer no true security, and they bind us to things that don't last.

Hebrews 6:13–19 tells us of the security of the salvation we have through Christ. This passage tells us that God desired so much to show us His purpose in our life is unchangeable, so He made a covenant. The Bible says that since God couldn't swear by anyone greater, He swore by Himself! And the promise that He swore to keep was for our salvation. Verses 18–19 tell us "so that by two unchangeable things in which it is impossible for God to lie (His promise and His oath), we who have taken refuge would have strong encouragement to take hold of the hope set before us. This hope we have as an anchor of the soul, a hope both sure and steadfast and one which enters within the veil (into the presence of God)" (parentheses added).

Do you see how much God desires you to be in His presence? He made a way through Christ—an Anchor for our very souls—so that we would be sure and steadfast and so that we can know without a doubt that He will never break His covenant of love with us. Where else in this world can we find such love and such desire for us? The psalmist wrote, "Whom have I in Heaven but You? And besides You, I desire nothing on earth. My flesh and my heart may fail, but God is the strength of my heart and my portion forever" (Ps. 73:25–26).

As we close out our study of these soul anchors, I wonder, What are you holding on to in your life? And what is holding on to you? Maybe as you've gone through this study, you have recognized a deep need in your heart and in your life for a Savior. If that is the case, I encourage you to pray a simple prayer, confessing to God that you recognize that you are in bondage of sin and that you know that Christ's sacrificial death on the cross of Calvary is the only thing that can break that bondage. Ask Him to forgive your sins, to break the chains that are binding you, and to come into your heart and your life to be your Savior and your Lord so that you can live with Him now and in eternity in Heaven. Making this commitment isn't going to fix every problem in your life, and it isn't going to suddenly fill you with all the answers. But connecting to the Anchor of your soul, Jesus Christ, will fill you with a sense of security, with hope, and with peace, such as you've never known before, and that you can't find in any other source on this earth. You will find in Him that one thing that is stronger than you that you can lean into and be held by when life throws its obstacles in your path.

Perhaps you have realized that you have tried to replace the anchors that Christ offers with the substitutes of this world. I hope that as you have read and studied these chapters, you have taken to heart all the promises that God's Word holds for you and remembered all the wonderful things that He has in store for His children. Even if you feel like you have lost your grip on Him, I hope that you have been reminded that He has never lost His grip on you and that you have gained the assurance that He never will.

References

Bridges, Jerry. 2007. *Respectable Sins: Confronting the Sins We Tolerate.* Colorado Springs: NavPress.

Lewis, C. S. 1962. *The Problem of Pain.* New York: Collier Books.

Lewis, C. S. 2001. *Mere Christianity.* San Francisco: Harper Collins.

MacArthur, John. 2006. The MacArthur Study Bible, NASB Updated Edition. La Habra, California: The Lockman Foundation.

Manning, Brennan. 1990. *The Ragamuffin Gospel.* Colorado Springs: Multnomah Publishers.

Tchividjian, Tullian. 2013. *One Way Love: Inexhaustible Grace for an Exhausted World.* Colorado Springs: David C. Cook Publishers.

Youssef, Michael. 2013. "The Rope of Life." ltw.org.

CPSIA information can be obtained at www.ICGtesting.com
Printed in the USA
LVOW07s0421010716

494829LV00002B/5/P